Travel Guide

TOKYO
TODAY

英文東京おもしろガイド

Nihombashi Bridge

Travel Guide

TOKYO
TODAY

Sightseeing
Activities
Eating & Drinking
Shopping
Accommodation & Health

英文東京おもしろガイド

First edition : January 1991

Edited by Japan Travel Bureau, Inc.
Editing Cooperation by Urban Translation Inc.
Maps by Kiyotomo Yamaguchi
Illustrations by Shinsaku Sumi
Photographs by Lee Ward Inc.
Translated by Julia Nolet, Martha Chaiklin, Urban Connections Inc.

Published by Japan Travel Bureau, Inc.

Printed in Japan

Introduction

This book aims to serve as a guide to life in Tokyo for English-speaking people, whether on a short vacation or a longer stay. Tokyo today is a rapidly expanding megalopolis, a major economic, commercial, and cultural center. An enjoyable stay for the foreign visitor or resident requires a careful selection from the vast resources available. For while Tokyo can truly be described as "the city that has everything," this can also make it difficult to decide where to begin: there are simply too many choices. If this book can simply help you avoid the immediate pitfalls of deciding where to dine, or shop, or seek out art and culture, we will consider our job a success. We would like to express our appreciation to many cultural facilities, theaters, shops, restaurants, and other institutions and organizations who generously cooperated to help us compile this volume.

CONTENTS

SIGHTSEEING
ACTIVITIES
EATING & DRINKING
SHOPPING
ACCOMMODATION & HEALTH
USEFUL INFORMATION

LEGEND

Structure **S** Shop   **H** Hotel
Greens   **R** Restaurant   **jtb** JTB Branch
JR   **E** Entertainment
Subway   **M** Museum

☎ Telephone number
S Nearest subway station
JR Nearest JR station
P Nearest private railway station
🕐 Business hours
H Weekly holiday
¥ Rate ★:2,000yen~ ★★:2,000~5,000yen
        ★★★:5,000~10,000yen ★★★★:10,000yen~
C Credit Cards JCB=JCB CARD
        DN=DINERS CLUB VISA=VISA CARD
        MC=MASTER CARD
        AMEX=AMERICAN EXPRESS CARD

English Name   Map Page
↓   ↓

| JENA FOREIGN BOOK STORE | 12 |
| イエナ洋書店　　　　 Iena yoshoten | C3 |

Japanese Name   Pronunciation   Map Location

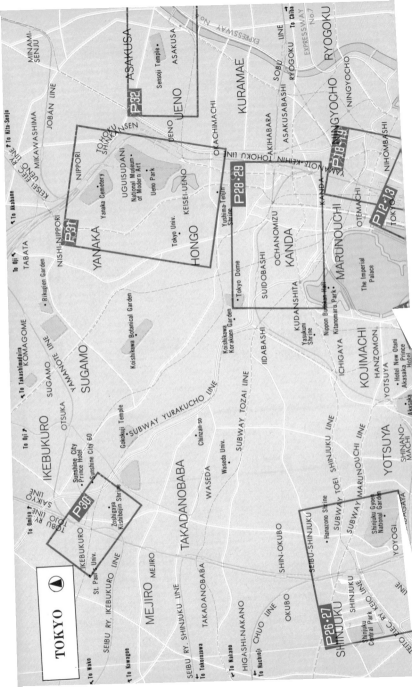

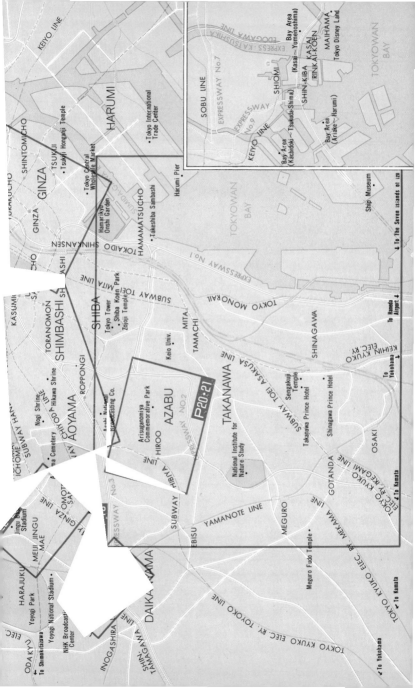

TRANSPORTATION OF TOKYO

SUBWAY TOEI MITA LINE
NISHI-TAKASHIMADAIRA
SHIN-TAKASHIMADAIRA
TAKASHIMADAIRA
NISHIDAI
HASUNE
SHIMURA-SANCHOME
SHIMURA-SAKAUE
HON-HASUNUMA
ITABASHI-HONCHO
ITABASHI-KUYAKUSHO

TOBU-TOJYO LINE
SHINRIN-KOEN
WAKO-SHI
EIDAN-NARIMASU
EIDAN-AKATSUKA
HEIWADAI
HIKAWADAI
KOTAKE-MUKAIHARA
SENKAWA
KANAMECHO
IKEBUKURO
OTSUKA
YAMANOTE LINE

SHIN-SAKURADAI
SEIBU R.Y. IKEBUKURO LINE
SHIN-OTSUKA
MYOGADANI
KORAKUEN

SEIBU R.Y. SHINJUKU LINE
MEJIRO
HIGASHI-IKEBUKURO
WASEDA
EDOGAWABASHI
GOKOKUJI
SUBWAY MARUNOUCHI LINE

MITAKA
KICHIJOJI
NISHI-OGIKUBO
OGIKUBO
ASAGAYA
KOENJI
NAKANO
OCHIAI
WASEDA
KAGURAZAKA
IIDABASHI
KUDANSHITA

MINAMI-ASAGAYA
SHIN-KOENJI
HIGASHI-KOENJI
SHIN-NAKANO
HIGASHI-NAKANO
OKUBO
TAKADANOBABA
SHIN-OKUBO
SEIBU-SHINJUKU
AKEBONOBASHI
ICHIGAYA
KOJIMACHI
HANZOMON

NAKANO-SAKAUE
NAKANO-SHIMBASHI
NAKANO-FUJIMICHO
SHINJUKU-SANCHOME
SHINJUKU-GYOENMAE
YOTSUYA-SANCHOME
YOTSUYA
NAGATACHO

SHIMO-TAKAIDO
HOHNANCHO
MEIDAI-MAE
SASAZUKA
HATAGAYA
HATUDAI
SHINJUKU
SHINANOMACHI
AOYAMA-ITCHOME
AKASAKA-MITSUKE
SAKURADAMON

HASHIMOTO
CHOFU
TOKYO-KYUKO ELEC. R.Y. SETAGAYA LINE
SHIMO-KITAZAWA
YOGI
SENDAGAYA
GAIENMAE
KOKKAIGIJIDOMAE

YOYOGI-UEHARA
HARAJUKU
MEIJI-JINGUMAE
NOGIZAKA
AKASAKA
KASUMIGASEKI

HON-ATSUGI
KEIO-TEITO ELEC. R.Y. INOKASHIRA LINE
YOYOGI-KOEN
SUBWAY HANZOMON LINE
OMOTE-SANDO
UCHISAIWAICHO

CHUO-RINKAN
TOKYO-KYUKO ELEC. R.Y. SHIN-TAMAGAWA LINE
FUTAKO-TAMAGAWAEN
YOGA
SAKURA-SHINMACHI
KOMAZAWA-DAIGAKU
SANGENJAYA
IKEJIRI-OHASHI
SHIBUYA
TORANOMON

KIKUNA
TAMAGAWAEN
DEN-EN-CHOFU
JIYUGAOKA
NAKA-MEGURO
EBISU
SUBWAY HIBIYA LINE
MEGURO
HIROO
ROPPONGI
KAMIYACHO

OHOKAYAMA
TOKYO-KYUKO ELEC. R.Y. MEKAMA LINE
ONARIMON
SHIBA-KOEN
SHINBASHI

HATANODAI
TOKYO-KYUKO ELEC. R.Y. IKEGAMI LINE
GOTANDA
TAKANAWADAI
DAIMON
SUBWAY TOEI MITA LINE

NISHI-MAGOME
MAGOME
TOEI NAKANOBU
TOGOSHI
OSAKI
SENGAKUJI
MITA

IKEGAMI
TOKYO-KYUKO ELEC. R.Y. OIMACHI LINE
HAMAMATSUCHO

KAMATA
OMORI
OIMACHI
SHINAGAWA
TAMACHI

KEIKYUKAMATA
KEIHIN-KYUKO ELEC. R.Y.
HANEDA
HANEDA-KUKO
TOKYO MONORAIL

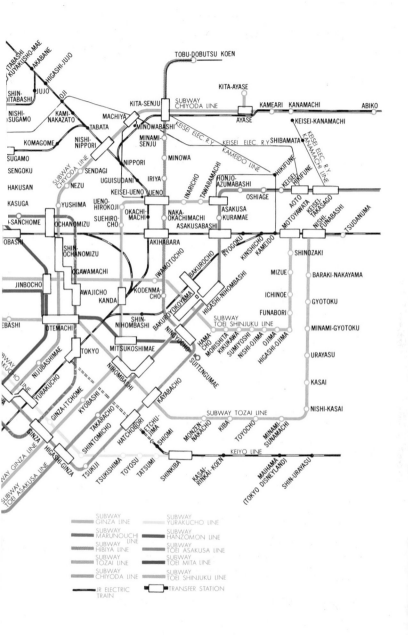

Transport and Communications

Using the Trains

● The Subway

The most convenient means of transport around central Tokyo is the city's subway system. There are actually two separate systems: the Eidan lines, run by a public corporation, and the Toei lines, under the administration of the Tokyo Metropolitan Government. The Eidan comprises seven lines: Ginza, Marunouchi, Hibiya, Tozai, Chiyoda, Yurakucho, and Hanzomon. Toei operates just three lines: Asakusa, Mita, and Shinjuku. Virtually any point in central Tokyo is within easy walking distance of a station on at least one of these lines.

What makes Tokyo's subway something of a challenge, however, is the complexity of the various routes. Even long-time Japanese residents of the city occasionally make mistakes, for example, in transferring from one line to another. Fares start at ¥140 on the Eidan and ¥140 on the Toei. Tickets are purchased from automatic vending machines, and include combination tickets good for passage on both systems.

● JR

JR is the overall name for the group of private companies that took over operation of the state-run Japan National Railways system several years ago. There are five JR lines in the Tokyo area: the Yamanote Line (silver cars with a light green stripe), which circles the city center; the Chuo (orange cars) and Sobu (yellow cars) Lines, which run east-west across the city; the Keihin Line (light blue cars), which parallels the Yamanote Line between Tabata and Shinagawa Stations; and the Saikyo Line (silver cars with a green stripe), running from Shinjuku into neighboring Saitama Prefecture. Most useful of these is the Yamanote Line. The 29 stations on this line include the important terminals of Shinjuku, Shibuya, Ikebukuro, Tokyo, and Ueno. Trains cover the entire loop in one hour, and during the daytime run at intervals of just a few minutes. JR fares start at ¥120. Travel between even the most distant stations on the Yamanote Line will cost no more than ¥180. Tickets are sold

both by vending machines and at windows. A newer innovation is the JR "Orange Card", a prepaid card that you can insert into ticket machines instead of cash.

● **Other Lines**

A number of other privately operated lines radiate outward from various stations on the JR Yamanote Line. These include the Keio, Odakyu, and Seibu Shinjuku Lines from Shinjuku; the Tokyu Toyoko, Tokyu Shintamagawa, and Keio Inokashira Lines from Shibuya; and the Seibu Ikebukuro and Tobu Tojo Lines from Ikebukuro. These private lines are useful when traveling to places on the outskirts of the city.

Using Taxis

No special cautions are required in using the taxis in Tokyo. They cruise throughout the city, and are easily recognized by their distinctive colors and roof signs. Fares are as indicated on the meter (a basic charge of ¥540 plus ¥80 for each 355m). Tipping is not customary, and —— the wonderful feature about Japanese cabs —— drivers are invariably honest about the fares. But this isn't to say that all is roses. It can be difficult to find a free taxi in entertainment districts at night.

On weekends in particular, just after the trains have stopped running, catching the first cab that comes along qualifies as almost a miracle. Also note that on crowded nights around train stations and other places with a marked taxi stand, you are expected to wait in line. If your destination is an obvious one, like "Roppongi" or "Hotel Okura", you can simply tell the driver. If lesser known, you should bring a map, written in Japanese, showing where it is.

Using the Buses

Buses serve every important train station in Tokyo. Their routes cover a countless number of stops, and used skillfully, they can be extremely convenient. City buses charge a fixed fare of ¥160; buses run by the several private companies in Tokyo charge ¥180. On either, after boarding the bus, you deposit the proper change or a ticket (available at train stations, bus offices, or on the bus

itself) into the fare box beside the driver. When you hear the name of your stop announced, press the button near your seat to sound the buzzer so that the driver will know to stop. Routes are confusing to the uninitiated, so you should study the map at the station bus terminal. To catch at any of the stops along a route, simply stand by the bus stop sign.

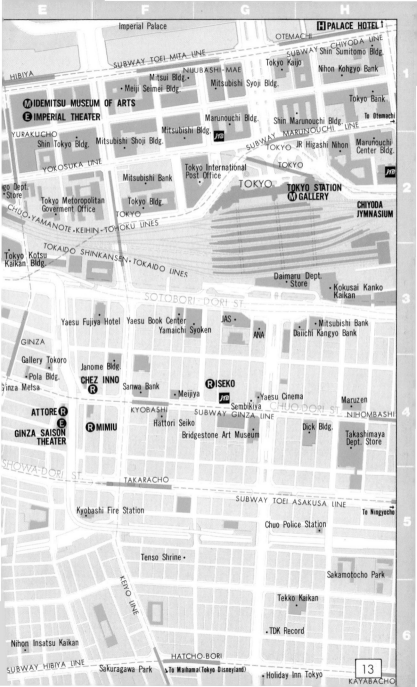

Imperial Palace

H PALACE HOTEL

OTEMACHI

E

F

G

H

SUBWAY TOEI MITA LINE

SUBWAY Shin Sumitomo Bldg. CHIYODA LINE

NIJUBASHI-MAE

Tokyo Kaijo

Nihon Kohgyo Bank

HIBIYA

Mitsui Bldg.

Mitsubishi Syoji Bldg.

Meiji Seimei Bldg.

Tokyo Bank

M IDEMITSU MUSEUM OF ARTS

E IMPERIAL THEATER

Marunouchi Bldg.

Shin Marunouchi Bldg.

To Otemachi

YURAKUCHO

Mitsubishi Bldg.

SUBWAY MARUNOUCHI LINE

Marunouchi

Shin Tokyo Bldg. Mitsubishi Shoji Bldg.

TOKYO JR Higashi Nihon

Center Bldg.

YOKOSUKA LINE

Mitsubishi Shoji Bldg.

TOKYO

JTB

Mitsubishi Bank

Tokyo International

TOKYO

TOKYO STATION

Post Office

M GALLERY

Tokyo Metoroplitan

Goverment Office

Tokyo Bldg.

TOKYO

CHIYODA

JYMNASIUM

CHUO-YAMANOTE-KEIHIN-TOHOKU LINES

go Dept.

Store

JTB

TOKAIDO SHINKANSEN-TOKAIDO LINES

Tokyo Kotsu

Kaikan Bldg.

Daimaru Dept.

Store

Kokusai Kanko

Kaikan

SOTOBORI-DORI ST.

Yaesu Fujiya Hotel Yaesu Book Center

JAS

Mitsubishi Bank

GINZA

Yamaichi Syoken

ANA

Daiichi Kangyo Bank

Gallery Tokoro

Janome Bldg.

Pola Bldg.

CHEZ INNO

R ISEKO

Ginza Melsa

R

Sanwa Bank

Meijiya

JTB

Yaesu Cinema

Maruzen

ATTORE R

Sembikiya

CHUO-DORI ST

NIHOMBASHI

KYOBASHI

SUBWAY GINZA LINE

E

R MIMIU

Hattori Seiko

Dick Bldg.

Takashimaya

GINZA SAISON

THEATER

Bridgestone Art Museum

Dept. Store

SHOWA-DORI ST.

TAKARACHO

SUBWAY TOEI ASAKUSA LINE

Kyobashi Fire Station

To Ningyocho

Chuo Police Station

Tenso Shrine

Sakamotocho Park

KEIYO LINE

Tekko Kaikan

TDK Record

Nihon Insatsu Kaikan

HATCHO-BORI

13

SUBWAY HIBIYA LINE

Sakuragawa Park

To Maihama(Tokyo Disneyland)

Holiday Inn Tokyo

KAYABACHO

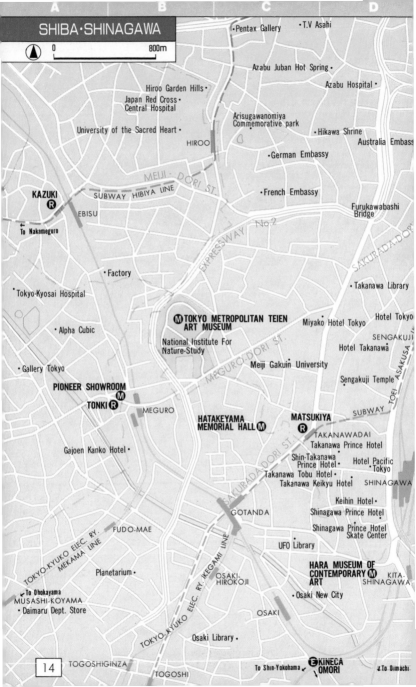

TOKYO PRINCE HOTEL

TOKYO TOWER AQUARIUM
TOKYO TOWER WAX MUSEUM

Shiba Park Hotel

DAIMON

abc Kaikan

Shiba Koen Park

SHIBAKOEN

SHIBA

Tokyo Grand Hotel

Kasuga Ryokan

CHUGOKU-HANTEN

Chisan Hotel Hamamatsucho

eio University

MITA

MATSUSHITA DENKO
LIFE SKETCH PLAZA

a Library

holta OA
ow Room

Mitsubishi Auto Garden

TAMACHI

ako
Tokyo

MINATO-KU SPORTS CENTER

GOLD

Hamarikyu-Onshi Garden

Water Surface

HAMAMATSUCHO

Bus Station

Old Shibarikyu-Onshi Garden

Takeshiba-Sanbashi

Hinode Pier Station

Home Design Center

Harumi Ground

TOKAIDO LINE

YAMANOTE·KEIHINTOHOKU

TOKYO

SHIBAURA
SAMBASHI

HARBOR

TOKAIDO SHINKANSEN

EXPRESSWAY No.1

Water Police Station

Kokuyo Tokyo Show Room

TOKYO MONORAIL

SHINAGAWA

SHINAGAWA
FUTO

Shinagawa Minami Futoh Park

SOUND COLOSSEUM
MZA

ARIAKE THE FOREST OF
TENNIS PARK

MUSEUM OF MARITIME SCIENCE

MBABA

To Haneda

KURHAUS HEIWAJIMA

SHOWA-NO-MORI TENNIS COURT

15

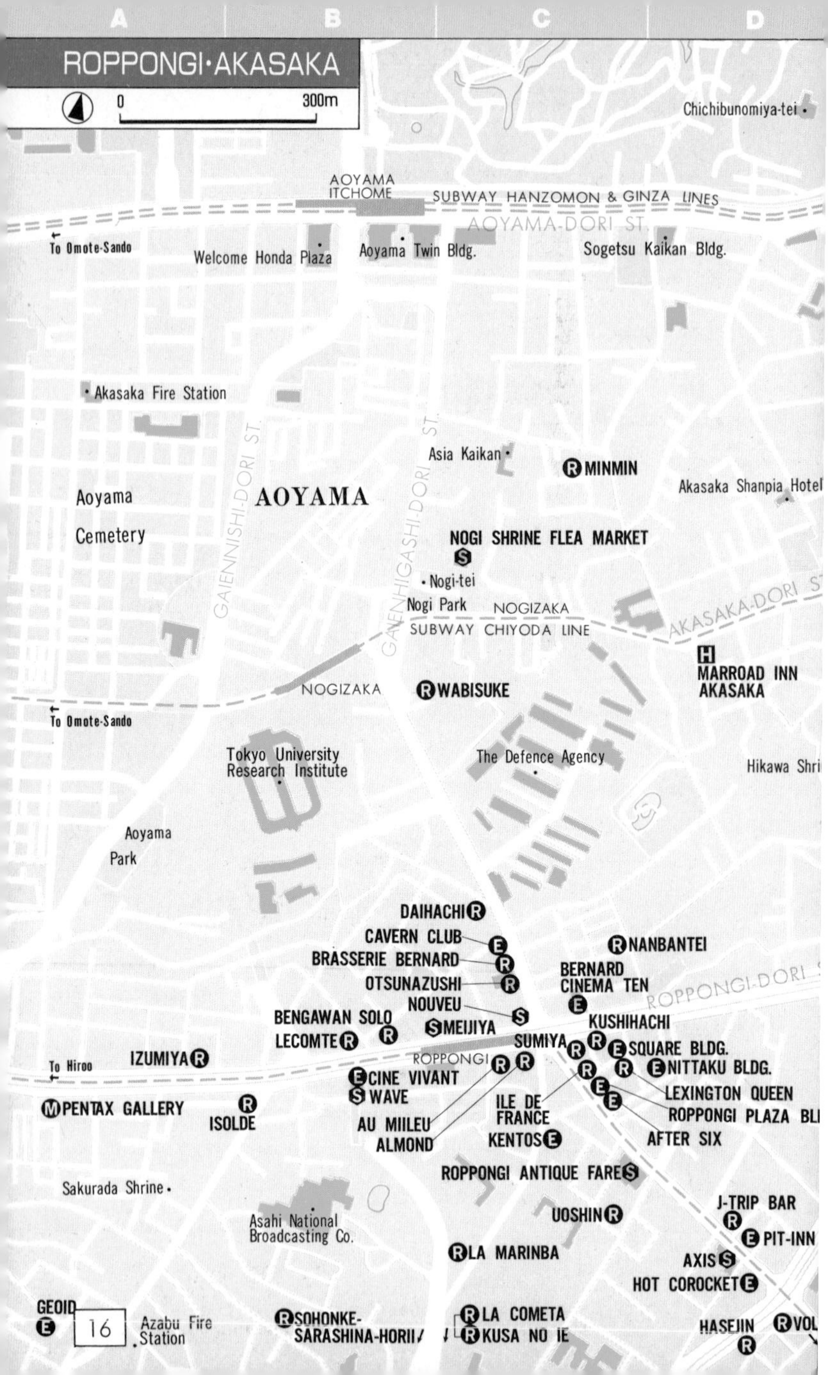

0   300m

Chichibunomiya-tei

AOYAMA
ITCHOME

SUBWAY HANZOMON & GINZA LINES
AOYAMA-DORI ST.

To Omote-Sando

Welcome Honda Plaza   Aoyama Twin Bldg.   Sogetsu Kaikan Bldg.

Akasaka Fire Station

Asia Kaikan

Ⓡ MINMIN

Akasaka Shanpia Hotel

Aoyama
Cemetery

AOYAMA

NOGI SHRINE FLEA MARKET
Ⓢ
・Nogi-tei

Nogi Park   NOGIZAKA
SUBWAY CHIYODA LINE

AKASAKA-DORI ST.

GAIENNISHI-DORI ST.

GAIENHIGASHI-DORI ST.

NOGIZAKA   Ⓡ WABISUKE

Ⓗ
**MARROAD INN
AKASAKA**

To Omote-Sando

Tokyo University
Research Institute

The Defence Agency

Hikawa Shri

Aoyama
Park

DAIHACHI Ⓡ

CAVERN CLUB Ⓔ

BRASSERIE BERNARD Ⓡ

OTSUNAZUSHI Ⓡ

Ⓡ **NANBANTEI**

**BERNARD
CINEMA TEN**
Ⓔ

ROPPONGI-DORI S

NOUVEU Ⓢ

BENGAWAN SOLO Ⓢ **MEIJIYA**

LECOMTE Ⓡ Ⓡ

KUSHIHACHI

Ⓡ Ⓡ Ⓔ **SQUARE BLDG.**
SUMIYA Ⓡ Ⓡ Ⓔ **NITTAKU BLDG.**

IZUMIYA Ⓡ

To Hiroo

ROPPONGI Ⓡ Ⓡ
Ⓡ Ⓔ
Ⓔ

LEXINGTON QUEEN
ROPPONGI PLAZA BLI

Ⓜ **PENTAX GALLERY**

Ⓔ **CINE VIVANT**
Ⓢ **WAVE**

ISOLDE Ⓡ

AU MIILEU
ALMOND

**ILE DE
FRANCE**

KENTOS Ⓔ

AFTER SIX

ROPPONGI ANTIQUE FARE Ⓢ

Sakurada Shrine ・

Asahi National
Broadcasting Co.

UOSHIN Ⓡ

J-TRIP BAR
Ⓡ
Ⓔ **PIT-INN**

Ⓡ **LA MARINBA**

AXIS Ⓢ
HOT COROCKET Ⓔ

Ⓔ
GEOID
16   Azabu Fire
Station

Ⓡ **SOHONKE-
SARASHINA-HORII**

Ⓡ **LA COMETA**
Ⓡ **KUSA NO IE**

HASEJIN Ⓡ **VOL**
Ⓡ

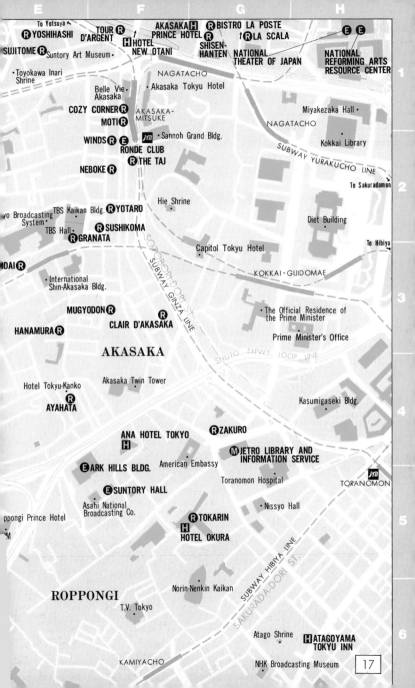

To Yotsuya

Ⓡ YOSHIHASHI
Ⓡ SUJITOME
TOUR D'ARGENT Ⓡ
Ⓗ HOTEL NEW OTANI
Suntory Art Museum •
AKASAKA Ⓗ PRINCE HOTEL
Ⓡ BISTRO LA POSTE
†Ⓡ LA SCALA
Ⓔ Ⓔ
SHISEN-HANTEN Ⓡ
NATIONAL THEATER OF JAPAN
NATIONAL REFORMING ARTS RESOURCE CENTER

• Toyokawa Inari Shrine

NAGATACHO

Belle Vie • Akasaka
• Akasaka Tokyu Hotel

Miyakezaka Hall •

COZY CORNER Ⓡ
MOTI Ⓡ
AKASAKA-MITSUKE

NAGATACHO

WINDS Ⓡ Ⓔ
Ⓙ • Sannoh Grand Bldg.
RONDE CLUB
Ⓡ THE TAJ

Kokkai Library

SUBWAY YURAKUCHO LINE

NEBOKE Ⓡ

To Sakuradamon

Hie Shrine

o Broadcasting System •
TBS Kaikan Bldg. Ⓡ YOTARO
TBS Hall •
Ⓡ SUSHIKOMA
Ⓡ GRANATA

Diet Building

ＤＡＩ Ⓡ

To Hibiya

• International Shin-Akasaka Bldg.

Capitol Tokyu Hotel

KOKKAI-GIJIDOMAE

SUBWAY GINZA LINE
SOTOBORI DORI ST.

MUGYODON Ⓡ
CLAIR D'AKASAKA Ⓡ

HANAMURA Ⓡ

• The Official Residence of the Prime Minister

Prime Minister's Office

AKASAKA

SHUTO EXPWY LOOP LINE

Akasaka Twin Tower

Hotel Tokyu-Kanko
Ⓡ AYAHATA

Kasumigaseki Bldg.

ANA HOTEL TOKYO Ⓗ
Ⓡ ZAKURO

Ⓜ JETRO LIBRARY AND INFORMATION SERVICE

Ⓔ ARK HILLS BLDG.
American Embassy

Ⓙ TORANOMON

Ⓔ SUNTORY HALL

Toranomon Hospital

Asahi National Broadcasting Co.

ppongi Prince Hotel
M

• Nissyo Hall

Ⓡ TOKARIN
Ⓗ HOTEL OKURA

SUBWAY HIBIYA LINE

ROPPONGI

Norin-Nenkin Kaikan

T.V. Tokyo

SAKURADA-DORI ST.

Atago Shrine
Ⓗ ATAGOYAMA TOKYU INN

KAMIYACHO

NHK Broadcasting Museum

17

NIHOMBASHI·
KYOBASHI·YAESU

0   200m

TOKYO STATION HOTEL — • Tokyo Station Hotel

SOBU LINE

TOKAIDO LINE

TOKAIDO SHINKANSEN LINE

TOKYO

EITAI-DORI ST

SOTOBORI · DORI ST.

• Daimaru Dept. Store

• Yaesu Book Center

Kokusai Kanko Kaikan

JAS

ANA

Daiichi kangyo Bank

~Ⓡ KYOTO YUTAKA

Fuji Bank   Sumitomo Shintaku Bank

Nihon Shinpan

Fuji Bldg.

• Kyodo Bldg.

Ⓡ ISEKO   Kyowa Bank

YAESU

Hotel Ryumeikan

• Ajinomoto Headquarters

• Taiyo-Kobe-Mitsui Bank

Sumitomo Kaijokasai Bldg.

Kyoritsu Bldg.

CHUO-DORI ST.

Nihon Shintaku

Asahi Seimei Kaikan

Bridgeston Art Museum

Yasuda Shintaku
Bank

Ⓢ MARUZEN

SHODOTEN

YAESU-DORI ST.

Taiyo-Kobe-Mitsui Bank

NIHOMBASHI

• Nichimen

Yaesu Bldg.

Yamamotoyama

KUROEYA

Takashimaya
Dept. Store

SUBWAY TOZAI LINE

• Uchida Yokoh

SHOWA · DORI ST.

HAIBARA Ⓢ

Mitsubishi Bank

SUBWAY TOEI ASAKUSA LINE

Taiyo Seimei Bldg.

Tokyu Dept.
Store

← To Ginza

Daiichi Kangyo Bank

Yokohama Bank

KITE MUSEUM Ⓜ

SHUTO EXPWY. LOOP LINE

Nissei Edobashi Bldg.

Daiwa Bank

Meiji Seimei

Ⓔ TOKYO ATRIUM
Ⓜ SAGACHO EXHIBIT SPACE
Ⓜ TOKYO STOCK EXCHANGE

18

Nihombashi Fire Station •

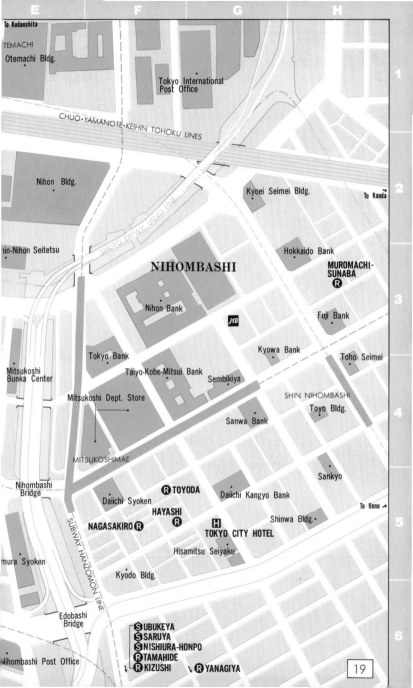

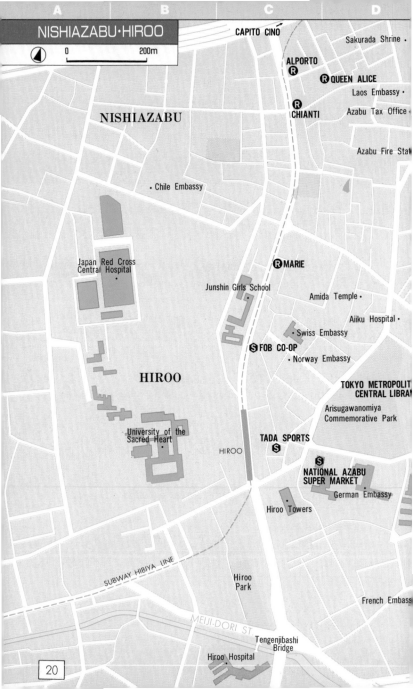

NISHIAZABU·HIROO

0   200m

CAPITO CINO

Sakurada Shrine .

ALPORTO
Ⓡ

Ⓡ **QUEEN ALICE**

Laos Embassy .

Ⓡ
CHIANTI

Azabu Tax Office .

Azabu Fire Sta

NISHIAZABU

. Chile Embassy

Ⓡ **MARIE**

Japan Red Cross
Central Hospital

Junshin Girls School
.

Amida Temple .

Aiiku Hospital .

. Swiss Embassy

Ⓢ **FOB CO-OP**

. Norway Embassy

HIROO

TOKYO METROPOLIT
CENTRAL LIBRA

Arisugawanomiya
Commemorative Park

University of the
Sacred Heart
.

TADA SPORTS
Ⓢ

HIROO

Ⓢ
NATIONAL AZABU
SUPER MARKET

German Embassy
.

Hiroo Towers
.

SUBWAY HIBIYA LINE

Hiroo
Park

French Embass

MEIJI-DORI ST

Tengenjibashi
Bridge

Hiroo Hospital

20

E F G H

Sweden Center •

Azabu Public Health Center

ou Sakurada Park

Azabu Library •

• Singapore Embassy

• Juban-Inari Shrine

AZABU-JUBAN •
HOT SPRING

Koryuji Temple •

Chinese Embassy

Austria Embassy •

NAGASAKA-
SARASHINA-HORII
Ⓡ

MOTOAZABU

Amishiro Park

• Halice Monument

Pakistani Embassy •

• Hikawa Shrine

Azabu Ground

Korean Embassy

i Univ.

• Finnish Embassy

MINAMI-AZABU

• Iranian Embassy

SHUTO EXPWY SHIBUYA LINE

Furukawabashi
Bridge

Ⓡ JINJU

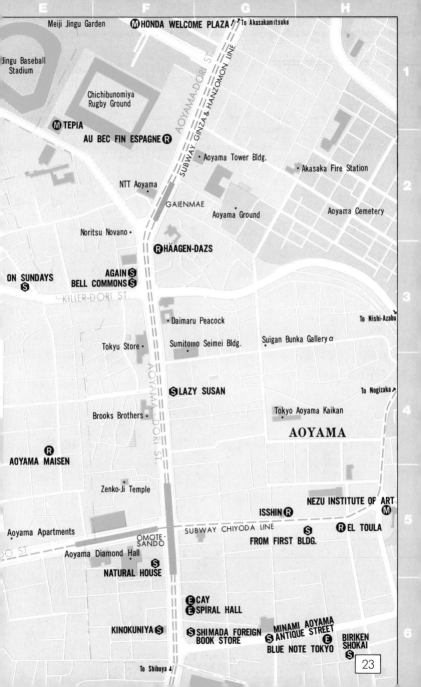

Meiji Jingu Garden

Jingu Baseball
Stadium

M HONDA WELCOME PLAZA / To Akasakamitsuke

Chichibunomiya
Rugby Ground

M TEPIA

AU BEC FIN ESPAGNE **R**

• Aoyama Tower Bldg.

• Akasaka Fire Station

NTT Aoyama •

GAIENMAE

Aoyama Ground •

Aoyama Cemetery

Noritsu Novano •

R HÄAGEN-DAZS

ON SUNDAYS
S

AGAIN **S**
BELL COMMONS **S**

KILLER-DORI ST.

• Daimaru Peacock

To Nishi-Azabu

Tokyu Store •

Sumitomo Seimei Bldg.

Suigan Bunka Gallery α

S LAZY SUSAN

To Nogizaka ⟋

Brooks Brothers •

Tokyo Aoyama Kaikan

AOYAMA

R
AOYAMA MAISEN

• Zenko-Ji Temple

NEZU INSTITUTE OF ART

ISSHIN **R**

M

Aoyama Apartments
•

SUBWAY CHIYODA LINE

S
FROM FIRST BLDG.

R EL TOULA

OMOTE-
SANDO

Aoyama Diamond Hall

S
NATURAL HOUSE

E CAY
E SPIRAL HALL

KINOKUNIYA **S**

S SHIMADA FOREIGN
BOOK STORE

MINAMI AOYAMA
S ANTIQUE STREET

BLUE NOTE TOKYO **E**

BIRIKEN
SHOKAI
S

To Shibuya ↓

23

0   200m

S NHK HALL

S GRAND'AILE

To Harajuku

**TEPCO ELECTRIC
ENERGY MUSEUM** **M**

NHK Broad Casting
· Center

Shibuya Public Hall

M
NHK TENJI PLAZA

Tax Office

Shibuya Ward Office

**TOBACCO AND
SALT MUSEUM**
M

BAMBOO COURT

Shibuya Tobu Hotel

HEICHINRO **R**

Worker's Welfare Hall ·

ZONART **S**

Parco Part 2 ·

INOKASHIRA-DORI ST.

KOEN-DORI ST.

Parco Part 1

NHK Kyodo Bldg.

Parco Part 3

S
TOKYU HANDS

S
SEIBU SEED

Shibuya Video Studio

S
TOWER RECORD

CINEMARISE **E**
SHIBUYA

SEIBU LOFT **S**

J-POP
E

BILLBOARD **R**

QUATTRO **E**

S ONE-OH-NINE

Kanze Noh Theater

ONE-OH-NINE 30'S **S**

TOKYU-HONTEN-DORI S

Tokyu Dept. Store

S
109

Toguri Art Museum

TOKYU BUNKAMURA **E**

R **BOUGAINVILLEA**
REIKYO **R**

The Prime

SHIN-TAMAGAWA LINE

DOGENZAKA

R **TARUYA**

PATTAYA **R**

KIRAKU **R**

Yamaha

DOGENZAKA-DORI ST.

INOKASHIRA LINE

S.I.JOE
E

Shoto Art Museum

SAKAE-DORI ST.

24

To Ikejiriohashi ↓

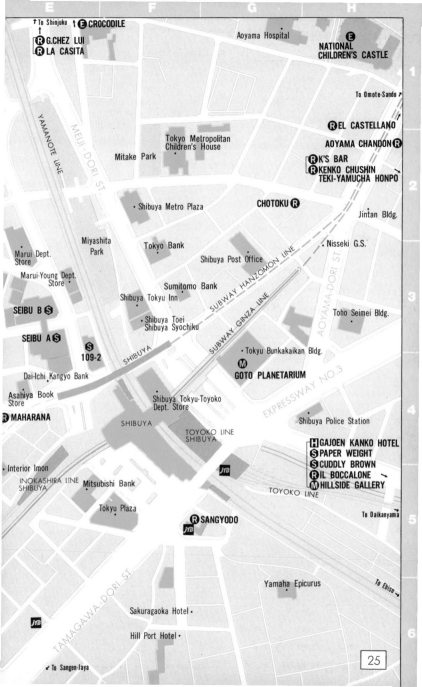

↑ To Shinjuku ↑ Ⓔ CROCODILE
Ⓡ G.CHEZ LUI
Ⓡ LA CASITA

Aoyama Hospital

Ⓔ NATIONAL CHILDREN'S CASTLE

To Omote-Sando ↗

Ⓡ EL CASTELLANO

AOYAMA CHANDON Ⓡ

Ⓡ K'S BAR
Ⓡ KENKO CHUSHIN TEKI-YAMUCHA HONPO

Tokyo Metropolitan Children's House

Mitake Park

YAMANOTE LINE

MEIJI-DORI ST.

Shibuya Metro Plaza

CHOTOKU Ⓡ

Jintan Bldg.

Miyashita Park

Tokyo Bank

Shibuya Post Office

Nisseki G.S.

Marui Dept. Store

Marui-Young Dept. Store

Sumitomo Bank

SUBWAY HANZOMON LINE

AOYAMA-DORI ST.

Toho Seimei Bldg.

SEIBU B Ⓢ

Shibuya Tokyu Inn

Shibuya Toei
Shibuya Syochiku

SUBWAY GINZA LINE

SEIBU A Ⓢ

Ⓢ 109-2

SHIBUYA

Tokyu Bunkakaikan Bldg.

Dai-Ichi Kangyo Bank

Ⓜ GOTO PLANETARIUM

Asahiya Book Store

EXPRESSWAY NO.3

Ⓡ MAHARANA

Shibuya Tokyu-Toyoko Dept. Store

SHIBUYA

Shibuya Police Station

TOYOKO LINE SHIBUYA

Ⓗ GAJOEN KANKO HOTEL
Ⓢ PAPER WEIGHT
Ⓢ CUDDLY BROWN
Ⓡ IL BOCCALONE
Ⓜ HILLSIDE GALLERY

Interior Imon

INOKASHIRA LINE SHIBUYA

Mitsubishi Bank

TOYOKO LINE

Tokyu Plaza

To Daikanyama →

JTB

Ⓡ SANGYODO

JTB

To Ebisu →

Yamaha Epicurus

TAMAGAWA-DORI ST.

JTB

Sakuragaoka Hotel •

Hill Port Hotel •

↙ To Sangen-Jaya

25

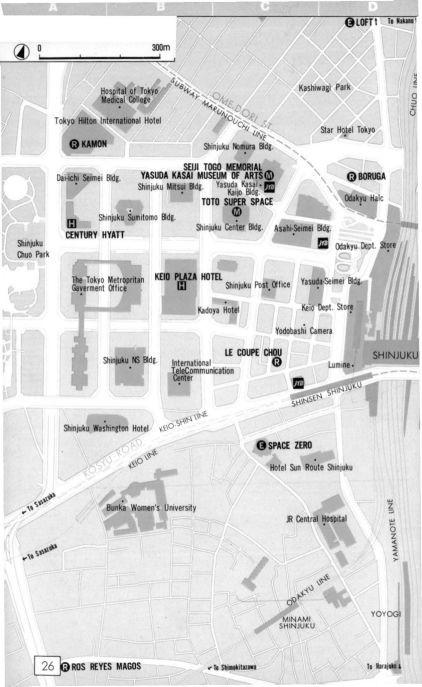

E LOFT 1   To Nakano 1

Hospital of Tokyo Medical College

Tokyo Hilton International Hotel

R KAMON

SUBWAY MARUNOUCHI LINE

OME-DORI ST.

Kashiwagi Park

Star Hotel Tokyo

CHUO LINE

Shinjuku Nomura Bldg.

Dai-ichi Seimei Bldg.

SEIJI TOGO MEMORIAL
YASUDA KASAI MUSEUM OF ARTS **M**

Shinjuku Mitsui Bldg.   Yasuda Kasai · Kaijo Bldg.

R BORUGA

Odakyu Halc

Shinjuku Sumitomo Bldg.

TOTO SUPER SPACE
M

Shinjuku Center Bldg.

Asahi-Seimei Bldg.

H
CENTURY HYATT

Odakyu Dept. Store

Shinjuku
Chuo Park

The Tokyo Metropritan
Gaverment Office

KEIO PLAZA HOTEL
H

Shinjuku Post Office

Yasuda-Seimei Bldg.

Kadoya Hotel

Keio Dept. Store

Yodobashi Camera

Shinjuku NS Bldg.

International
TeleCommunication
Center

LE COUPE CHOU
R

Lumine ·

SHINJUKU

SHINSEN SHINJUKU

Shinjuku Washington Hotel

KEIO-SHIN LINE

KOSYU ROAD

KEIO LINE

E SPACE ZERO

Hotel Sun Route Shinjuku

← To Sasazuka

← To Sasazuka

Bunka Women's University

JR Central Hospital

YAMANOTE LINE

ODAKYU LINE

MINAMI
SHINJUKU

YOYOGI

26   **R** ROS REYES MAGOS

← To Shimokitazawa

To Harajuku ↓

0   300m

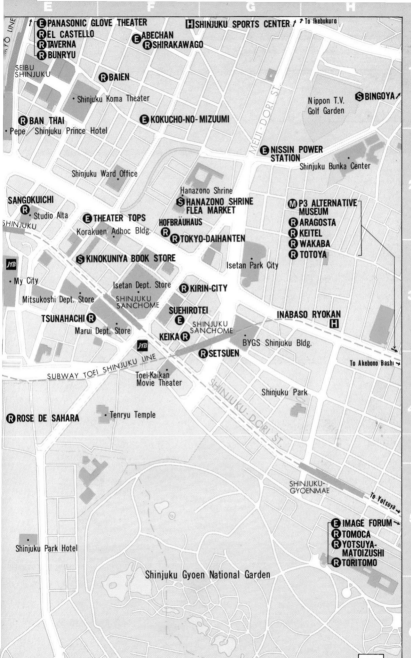

E PANASONIC GLOVE THEATER
R EL CASTELLO
R TAVERNA
R BUNRYU

E ABECHAN
R SHIRAKAWAGO

H SHINJUKU SPORTS CENTER

↗ To Ikebukuro

SEIBU
SHINJUKU

R BAIEN

• Shinjuku Koma Theater

MEIJI-DORI ST.

Nippon T.V.
Golf Garden

S BINGOYA

R BAN THAI
• Pepe / Shinjuku Prince Hotel

E KOKUCHO-NO-MIZUUMI

E NISSIN POWER
STATION

Shinjuku Bunka Center

Shinjuku Ward Office

Hanazono Shrine

S HANAZONO SHRINE
FLEA MARKET

SANGOKUICHI
R • Studio Alta

E THEATER TOPS
Korakuen Adhoc Bldg.

HOFBRÄUHAUS
R
R TOKYO-DAIHANTEN

M P3 ALTERNATIVE
MUSEUM
R ARAGOSTA
R KEITEL
R WAKABA
R TOTOYA

SHINJUKU

S KINOKUNIYA BOOK STORE

Isetan Park City

• My City

Isetan Dept. Store

R KIRIN-CITY

Mitsukoshi Dept. Store

SHINJUKU
SANCHOME

SUEHIROTEI
E

INABASO RYOKAN
H

R TSUNAHACHI

Marui Dept. Store

SHINJUKU
SANCHOME

BYGS Shinjuku Bldg.

KEIKA **R**

R SETSUEN

SUBWAY TOEI SHINJUKU LINE

Toei-Kaikan
Movie Theater

SHINJUKU-DORI ST.

Shinjuku Park

To Akebono Bashi →

R ROSE DE SAHARA

• Tenryu Temple

SHINJUKU-
GYOENMAE

To Yotsuya →

E IMAGE FORUM →
R TOMOCA
R YOTSUYA-
MATOIZUSHI
R TORITOMO

Shinjuku Park Hotel

Shinjuku Gyoen National Garden

↓ To Sendagaya   ↓ To Shibuya

27

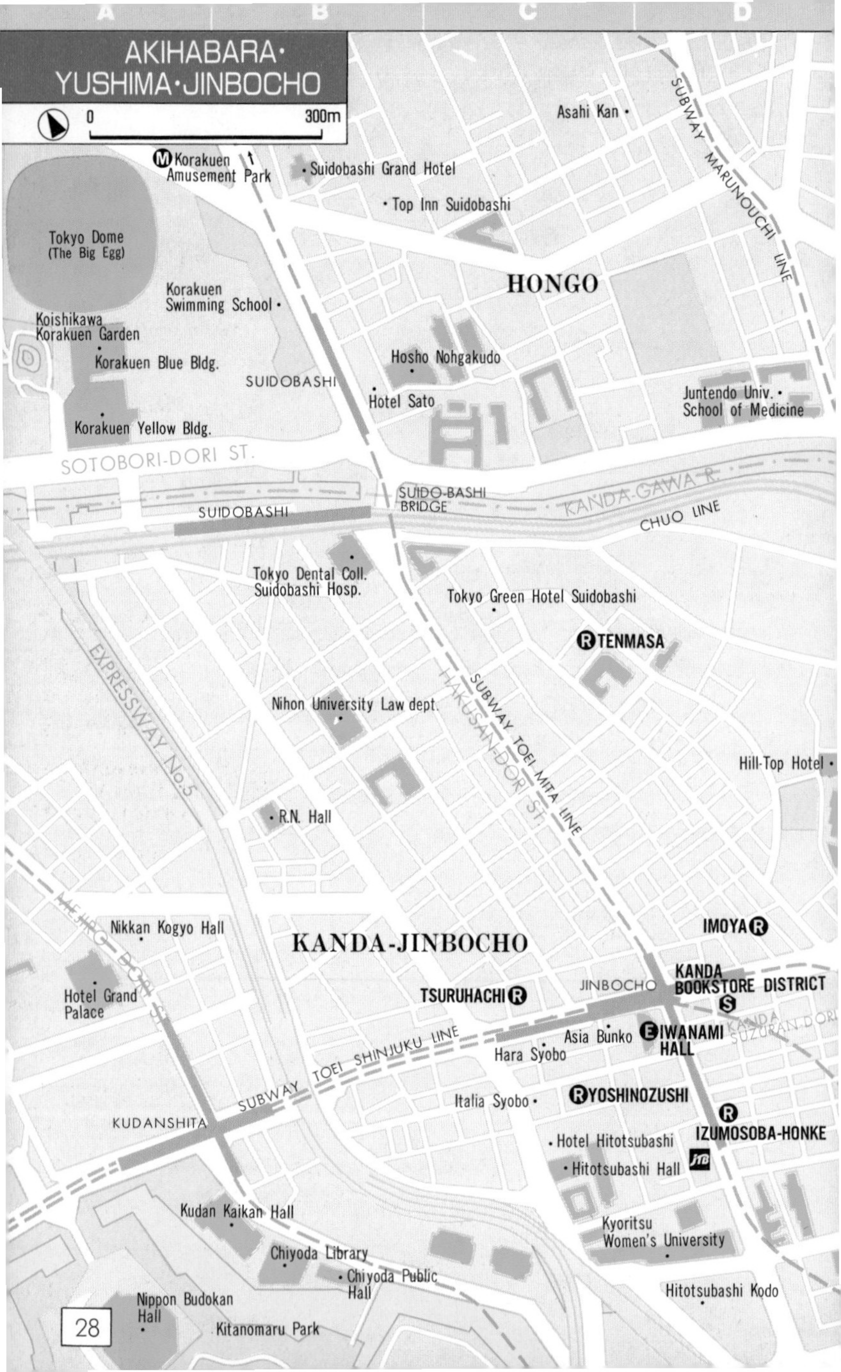

AKIHABARA·YUSHIMA·JINBOCHO

0   300m

Asahi Kan ·

SUBWAY MARUNOUCHI LINE

ⓂKorakuen Amusement Park

· Suidobashi Grand Hotel

· Top Inn Suidobashi

HONGO

Tokyo Dome (The Big Egg)

Korakuen Swimming School ·

Koishikawa Korakuen Garden

Korakuen Blue Bldg.

SUIDOBASHI

Hosho Nohgakudo

· Hotel Sato

Juntendo Univ. · School of Medicine

Korakuen Yellow Bldg.

SOTOBORI-DORI ST.

SUIDOBASHI

SUIDO-BASHI BRIDGE

KANDA-GAWA R.

CHUO LINE

Tokyo Dental Coll. Suidobashi Hosp.

Tokyo Green Hotel Suidobashi

Ⓡ TENMASA

EXPRESSWAY No.5

Nihon University Law dept.

SUBWAY TOEI MITA LINE

HAKUSAN-DORI ST.

Hill-Top Hotel ·

· R.N. Hall

MEHRO-DORI

· Nikkan Kogyo Hall

KANDA-JINBOCHO

IMOYA Ⓡ

JINBOCHO

KANDA BOOKSTORE DISTRICT

Hotel Grand Palace

TSURUHACHI Ⓡ

Ⓢ

Asia Bunko **Ⓔ IWANAMI HALL**

KANDA SUZURAN-DORI

SUBWAY TOEI SHINJUKU LINE

Hara Syobo

KUDANSHITA

Italia Syobo ·

Ⓡ YOSHINOZUSHI

Ⓡ

IZUMOSOBA-HONKE

· Hotel Hitotsubashi 🆖

· Hitotsubashi Hall

Kudan Kaikan Hall

Kyoritsu Women's University

Chiyoda Library

· Chiyoda Public Hall

Hitotsubashi Kodo

28

Nippon Budokan Hall

Kitanomaru Park

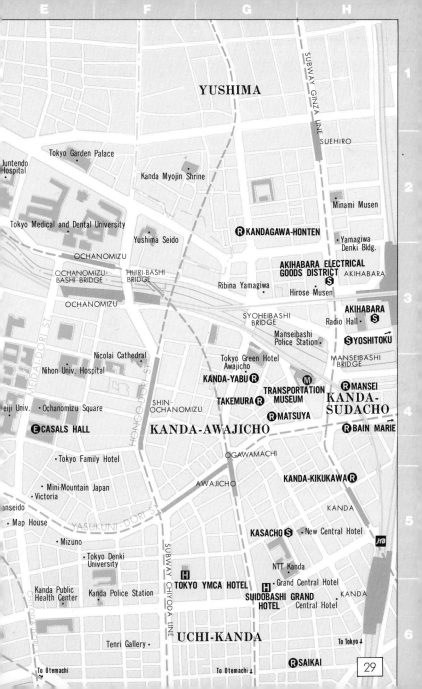

YUSHIMA

SUEHIRO

Juntendo
Hospital

Tokyo Garden Palace

Kanda Myojin Shrine

Minami Musen

Tokyo Medical and Dental University

Yushima Seido

·Yamagiwa
Denki Bldg.

Ⓡ KANDAGAWA-HONTEN

OCHANOMIZU

**AKIHABARA ELECTRICAL
GOODS DISTRICT** AKIHABARA

OCHANOMIZU·
BASHI BRIDGE

HIJIRI-BASHI
BRIDGE

Ribina Yamagiwa

Hirose Musen

OCHANOMIZU

AKIHABARA

Radio Hall · Ⓢ

SYOHEIBASHI
BRIDGE

Ⓢ YOSHITOKU

Nicolai Cathedral

Manseibashi
Police Station ·

MANSEIBASHI
BRIDGE

Nihon Univ. Hospital

Tokyo Green Hotel
Awajicho

KANDA-YABU Ⓡ

Ⓜ

Ⓡ MANSEI

·eiji Univ. · Ochanomizu Square

SHIN-
OCHANOMIZU

TAKEMURA Ⓡ

**TRANSPORTATION
MUSEUM**

**KANDA-
SUDACHO**

Ⓔ CASALS HALL

KANDA-AWAJICHO

Ⓡ MATSUYA

Ⓡ BAIN MARIE

· Tokyo Family Hotel

OGAWAMACHI

· Mini-Mountain Japan
· Victoria

AWAJICHO

KANDA-KIKUKAWA Ⓡ

anseido

KANDA

· Map House

YASUKUNI-DORI ST.

· Mizuno

KASACHO Ⓢ · New Central Hotel

· Tokyo Denki
University

SUBWAY CHIYODA LINE

NTT Kanda

Kanda Public
Health Center

Kanda Police Station

**H
TOKYO YMCA HOTEL**

H · Grand Central Hotel

**SUIDOBASHI GRAND
HOTEL** Central Hotel

KANDA

JTB

MEIDAI-DORI ST.

HONGO-DORI ST.

CHIYODA-DORI ST.

UCHI-KANDA

Tenri Gallery ·

To Tokyo ↓

To Otemachi

To Otemachi ↓

Ⓡ SAIKAI

29

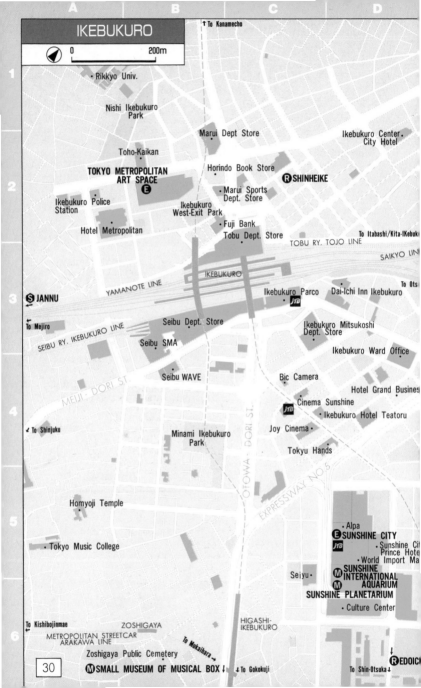

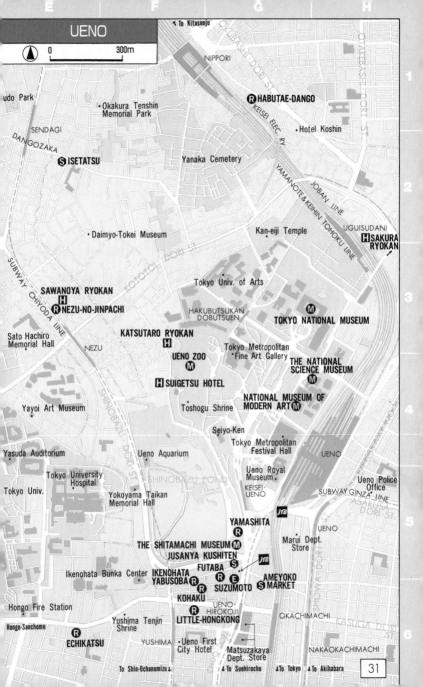

ASAKUSA

0   300m

- Kappa Temple

Yasaki Inari Shrine •

KAPPABASHI DORI ST.

S KONDO-SHOTEN

Tokyo Honganji Temple •

S

KAPPABASHI DISTRICT

KITCHEN SUPPLY

H KIKUYA RYOKAN

← **R YANAGIBASHI NINKI-YA**

Asakusa Bisuta Hotel •

TAWARAMACHI

• Asakusa Post Office

ASAKUSA IMAHAN
R

• Asakusa View Hotel

SUBWAY GINZA LINE

KOKUSAI-DORI

ROX

R
OWARIYA

• NTT Asakusa

E ASAKUSA ENGEI HALL

KOTOTOI-DORI ST.

To Yoshiwara Shrine

R ICHIMON

YONEKYU R

S ADACHIYA

KAMINARIMON-DORI ST.

ASAKUSA-DORI LINE

HANAYASHIKI
M

R KOMAGATA DOJO

ASAKUSA

YONOYA R DAIKOKUYA
MIKAWAYA BEKKAN S
H

• Dempoin Temple

H (SUKEROKU-NO YADO)
SADACHIYO (BEKKAN)

TOKIWA HALL
R
UMEMURA

Kaminari Gate

NAKAMISE-DORI ST.

S SUKEROKU

Sensoji Hospital •

KOMAGATA-BASHI BRIDGE

HOSENDO-KYUAMI S R

MASARU

S R

Sensoji Temple

ASAKUSA

R KAMIYA BAR

KUREMUTSU

• Asakusa Shrine

FUJIYA

R KATORI

Matsuya • Dept. Store

EDO-DORI ST.

TOBU ASAKUSA

Asakusa • Police Station

UMAMICHI-DORI ST.

AZUMA-BASHI BRIDGE

SUPER DRY HALL
R

SUBWAY TOEI ASAKUSA LINE

HONJO AZUMABASHI

TOBU RY. ISEZAKI LINE

Sumida Park

KOTOTOI-BASHI BRIDGE

Sumida Park

SUMIDA-GAWA R.

EXPRESSWAY NO.6

To Ishihama Shrine

SAKURA-BASHI BRIDGE

• Josenji Temple

NARIHIRABASHI

R KOTOTOI DANGO

Chomeiji Temple •

32   ↓ To Oshiage ↓

↘ To Matsudo

JTB For Your Travelife

ILLUSTRATED

JAPAN IN YOUR POCKET

SERIES

This cleary-illustrated
guide book series offer a wealth
of highly readable information
about this country on all aspects
of daily life, Tokyo, Kyoto,
festivals, lifestyle of "Salaryman,"
historical personages, etc.
viewed from various angles.

Vol. 1 A LOOK INTO JAPAN
Vol. 2 LIVING JAPANESE STYLE
Vol. 3 EATING IN JAPAN
Vol. 4 FESTIVALS OF JAPAN
Vol. 5 MUST-SEE IN KYOTO
Vol. 6 MUST-SEE IN NIKKO
Vol. 7 A LOOK INTO TOKYO
Vol. 8 "SALARYMAN" IN JAPAN
Vol. 9 WHO'S WHO OF JAPAN
Vol.10 TODAY'S JAPAN
Vol.11 REGARD SUR LE JAPON (French Version)
Vol.12 VIE AU JAPON (French Version)
Vol.13 JAPANESE CHARACTERS
Vol.14 JAPANESE INN AND TRAVEL

Vol.1 — Vol.14
910 — 1010 yen each
(tax included)

JAPAN TRAVEL BUREAU

PUBLISHING DIVISION

Oki Bldg. 8th Floor, 3-3 Kanda Ka,ji-cho Chiyoda-ku, Tokyo, Japan

An international whisky born from the love between a Japanese gentleman and a Scottish lady.

In spring of 1920, a young Japanese man who was studying to make whisky married a Scottish girl in Scotland. His name was Masataka Taketsuru, the founder of Nikka Whisky. The girl's name was Jessie Roberta Cowan. Despite her family's opposition, they got married and came to Japan where they devoted to formulation of real whisky. Even though they faced many hardships, they never gave up their dream of producing whisky.

At last in 1940, 20 years after they got married, the first Nikka Whisky was sold. Ever since Nikka has brought out many renowned whiskies to the world, and along with them their passion keeps on living.

SUPER NIKKA

SIGHTSEEING

Amusement parks, aquariums and planetariums
for the child in you....
Galleries and museums for the adult.

General Sightseeing Advice

Tokyo has neither the natural splendor of Hokkaido or Kyushu, nor the sheer number of famous shrines and temples of Kyoto and Nara. Walking the streets, the main impression is that of a huge, bustling city, filled with the noises of people and traffic. But for all that, this is the capital of Japan, and has been for the hundreds of years since the Tokugawa Shogunate. If you can look beyond the skyscrapers and the flashy stores, you will see a city abounding in culture and history. Tokyo can be divided into several major areas. There is old downtown, or *shitamachi* around Ueno and Asakusa. In contrast is the newer Yamanote "uptown" area, including Shinjuku, Shibuya, and Roppongi. Between these two is the Imperial Palace/Ginza area. Finally is the rapidly developing waterfront area along Tokyo Bay. Of these, Ueno and Asakusa are where you will find the echoes of the city Tokyo used to be. This has long been the neighborhood of the common Tokyoite, and both cultural artifacts and a general ambience remain. The Yamanote area, on the other hand, offers a modern cityscape. Here you will discover the city's most stylish shops and restaurants. The waterfront area is meanwhile home to Tokyo Disneyland and a number of other new cultural and entertainment facilities. Perhaps the best approach to understanding the totality of Tokyo today would be to start with its historic sites, then going on to its arts, its restaurants, and finally, its nightlife. But if that sounds too ambitious, decide what your own interests are, then seek them out. Even if you choose to concentrate on just one aspect of the city — its art, for example, or its nightlife —— you should find it a place of fascination and excitement.

Model Sightseeing Courses

Here we offer several suggested sightseeing itineraries around different parts of the city. Each is designed to be covered on foot. If you want to cover a wider expanse of the city at a time, make use of the subways, or call Sunrise Tours (☎ 3276-7777), a company which runs scheduled bus tours of the city.

● **Imperial Palace/Ginza Course**

This walk takes you around the heart of Tokyo, from the Imperial Palace and its historical memories to Hibiya Park, Tokyo's downtown refuge. Then on to Ginza, where you might want to browse among the department stores or take time out at a restaurant. Begin at Ⓢ Nijubashi Station → Imperial Palace Square → Nijubashi → Hibiya Park → Imperial Hotel → Yurakucho "Mullion" → Ginza (total distance: approximately 2km, about 1 hr.)

FANTASYLAND

TOMORROWLAND

WORLD BAZAAR

WESTERNLAND

ADVENTURELAND

A Variety of Events

Adding to the appeal of Tokyo Disneyland are the many daily and special events. From 3 pm. every day, Mickey Mouse, Donald Duck and other favorite Disney characters parade around the grounds. "Electrical Parades" in the evenings on weekends (except in winter) and on summer and winter holidays feature floats decorated with countless glowing lights. It's an unforgettable pageant of light and sound. Colorful events are also held on Christmas, New Year's Eve, and other special occasions.

Unique Shopping

Though overlooked by most visitors to Tokyo Disneyland, many unique souvenirs are offered for sale. Some 30,000 items are available, primarily related to Disney cartoon characters: Mickey Mouse dolls and caps, toys, candy, accessories, and so much more it can be difficult to make a choice. But don't worry about running out of money —— there's even a bank.

1-1 Maihama, Urayasu-shi, Chiba-ken ☎ 0473-54-0001 [JR] Maihama Sta./Direct bus services from [S] Urayasu Sta. [JR] Tokyo, Ueno, Yokohama Stations, Narita and Haneda Airports ⊙ Varies seasonally [H] Varies seasonally [¥] Adult 3,000, Child 2,000(Admission fee only)/ Passport: 4,400 (Admission plus free pass)/ Big 10: 4,100 (Admission plus 10 ride tickets)

TOSHIMAEN
としまえん

A 12-minutes train ride from Ikebukuro station, this amusement park is popular among young people for its many exciting rides (or "scream machines", as they're called here). There are attractions for every age from small children to adults — merry-go-rounds and other traditional rides; spiral, loop-the-loop, and various other roller coasters; and the "Flying Pirates"— a huge ship that ascends and then drops suddenly. Popular in the summer are the seven swimming pools, including ones with waves and ones with flowing water, and the huge "Hydropolis," entered by a water slide. Toshimaen is also renowned for its big fireworks show each Saturday night in midsummer.

3-25-1 Mukaiyama, Nerima-ku ☎ 3990-3131 P Seibu-Toshima Line Toshimaen Sta. ◷ 9:00-17:00 (hours vary seasonally) H None (Nov.-Mar: Wed.) ¥ Adult 1,600 Children 800 (Rides and attractions not included)

TOSHIMAEN

KORAKUEN AMUSEMENT PARK
後楽園ゆうえんち

28

A1

KORAKUEN

Next to the Tokyo Dome in the heart of the city, this amusement park is superbly located. The closest stations are JR Suidobashi and the Marunouchi subway line's Korakuen station. The favorite rides are of the white-knuckle variety:"UltraTwister" with its 85° slope and four high-speed loops: "Sky Flower" with their rapid 70-meter drop; and"Viking", a large boat that swings like a pendulum. Also popular here are live shows for children, featuring famed cartoon characters. After dark, the illuminated rides create a wonderland of moving lights.

1-8 Koraku, Bunkyo-ku☎3811-2111 S Korakuen Sta., S JR Suidobashi Sta. ◷ 10:00-19:00 (hours vary seasonally) H None ¥ Adult 1,100 Children 650 (Rides and attractions not included)

HANAYASHIKI

花やしき

Even Tokyoites are surprised to learn that Hanayashiki, located next to Asakusa's Sensoji Temple, dates back to Edo days. Then, however, it was a flower garden. The flowers remain, but are now joined by rides including Japan's first roller coaster, a merry- go-round, bumper cars, and exciting new attractions like the "TP-1 Instantaneous Transport Unit". A surprisingly colorful and modern place to find in the midst of old Asakusa, and an interesting stop before or after visiting the temple.

2-28-1 Asakusa, Taito-ku ☎ 3842-8780 Ⓢ Asakusa Sta. ◯ 10:00-18:00 (hours vary seasonally) Ⓗ None ¥ Adult 400 Children 200 (Rides and attractions not included)

HANAYASHIKI

TOKYO SESAME PLACE

東京セサミプレイス

A new type of amusement park, opened in the autumn of 1990 on a wooded hill over the Akikawa Hill on Tokyo's western edge. As the name suggests, this is a re-creation of the Sesame Street of television fame. Walk through an exact replica of the street and meet Big Bird and all the other characters — any fan of the TV program is assured a full day of fun.

403 Hatchoji, Ajiro, Itsukaichi-machi, Nishitama-gun ☎ 0425-96-5811 ⱼᴿ Akikawa Sta. ◯ hours vary seasonally Ⓗ Wed. ¥ Adult 2,100 Children 2,600 (Includes attractions)

TOKYO SESAME PLACE

UENO ZOO | 31

上野動物園 | Ueno Dobutsu-en | C4

Probably Japan's best known zoo, Ueno Zoo was also its first: it opened in 1882. Though located in the center of the city, it has preserved its large (140,000 sq.m) grounds, making it as much a place to stroll as to see animals. These grounds are divided into Eastern and Western areas. You enter through the Eastern, which features elephants, gorillas, bears, tigers, lions, and — the popular favorite — pandas from China. The Western part includes hippos, rhinos, giraffes, and zebras, as well as a mini-ranch and an aquarium.

9-83 Ueno-koen, Taito-ku ☎3828-5171 Ⓢ Ⓙ Ueno Sta. ⊙ 9:00-16:00 Ⓗ Mon. ¥ Adult 400 Jr. high students 100 Elementary school students and senior citizens free

UENO ZOO

TAMA ZOOLOGICAL PARK | –

多摩動物公園 | Tama Dobutsu-Koen | –

This zoo displays African and other animals from around the world in an environment somewhat closer to their natural habitat than most zoos in Japan. It takes advantage of a hilly, wooded 530,000 sq.m site — big enough for a full day's exploration. The park is divided into a number of areas, but is proudest of the koala bears in its Australian area. Only a handful of zoos in Japan have these extremely popular animals. Another

TAMA ZOOLOGICAL PARK

favorite is the lion park, in which some 20 varieties of lions roam freely (you tour it in the safety of a bus). On a smaller scale, the insect house features rare insects from every corner of the globe.

7-1-1 Hodokubo, Hino-shi ☎ 0425-91-1611 Ⓟ Keio Line Tama-dobutsu-koen Sta. ⊙ 9:30-16:00 Ⓗ Mon. ¥ Adult 400 Jr. high students 100 Elementary school students and Senior citizens free

TOKYO SEA LIFE PARK

葛西臨海水族園   **Kasai Rinkai Suizokuen**

Just one of the many new leisure facilities being developed along the Tokyo Bay waterfront, Kasai Rinkai Park opened in 1989. The park's main attraction is the Tokyo Sea Life Park aquarium in its own unique domed building. Inside is a huge donut-shaped tank featuring schools of tuna, as well as more than 300 other varieties of fish and marine life. The lecture room offers presentations using 3D imagery. An excellent place to learn more about the sea and the life within it.

Rinkai-cho, Edogawa-ku ☎ 3869-5151 JR Kasai-Rinkaikoen Sta. ◷ 9:30-16:00 H Mon. ¥ Adults:600, Children 13-15: 200, Senior citizens and children 12 and under: Free.

TOKYO SEA LIFE PARK

SUNSHINE INTERNATIONAL AQUARIUM   `30`

サンシャイン国際水族館   **Sunshine Suizoku-kan**   `D5`

Occupying the 10th and 11th floors of the World Import Center, next to the Sunshine 60 skyscraper in Ikebukuro, this is the world's first high-rise (40m) aquarium. The water, tank, lighting, and sound have nevertheless been designed to resemble a natural aquatic environment as closely as possible. The 20,000 sea creatures of 570 varieties include not only fish, but also sea otters, two-toned black and white "panda" dolphins, seals, and even penguins. Also enjoy feeding shows, sea lion shows, and a marine circus.

3-1-3 Higashi-Ikebukuro,Toshima-ku ☎ 3989-3466 S Higashi-Ikebukuro Sta. ◷ 10:00-18:00 (Sun. & hol. -18:30) H None ¥ Adult 1,440 Children 720

SUNSHINE INTERNATIONAL AQUARIUM

TOKYO TOWER AQUARIUM/TOKYO TOWER WAX MUSEUM | 15

東京タワー水族館・蠟人形館　Tokyo Tower Suizoku-kan/Tokyo Tower Ro Ningyo-kan | E1

For all Tokyo Tower's fame, the aquarium on its ground floor is surprisingly little known. Devoted to ornamental species, it houses some 50,000 fish of 800 beautiful varieties, divided by region of origin (South America, Africa, Europe, etc.). There is also a Japanese section, which includes varieties such as carp and goldfish. Next door is an equally interesting wax museum where you can see realistic replicas of some 120 famous people. They range from the contemporary (Michael Jackson) to the legendary (Marilyn Monroe) to the historical (post-war prime minister Shigeru Yoshida).

4-2-8 Shiba-koen, Minato-ku ⑤ Kamiyacho Sta., Onarimon Sta./Tokyo Tower Aquarium ☎3434-8833 ⏰ 10:00-19:00 (Hours vary seasonally) Ⓗ None ¥ 1,000/Tokyo Tower Wax Museum ☎ 3436-6661 ⏰ 10:00-19:00 Ⓗ None ¥ 750

TOKYO TOWER WAX MUSEUM

GOTO PLANETARIUM | 25

五島プラネタリウム | G3

Located in the Tokyo Bunka Kaikan building in Shibuya, this is a long-established and fairly orthodox planetarium. The regular program changes each month, to focus on the sky at that particular time of the year. A special presentation called "An Evening of Stars and Music" is given from 6 pm each Friday and Saturday. (Closed for renovations through Feb. 8, 1991)

Tokyu Bunka Kaikan, 2-21-12 Shibuya, Shibuya-ku ☎ 3407-7409 ⑤ JR Shibuya Sta. ⏰ 11:10-18:00 (Sat., Sun. & hol. 10:30-18:00) Ⓗ Mon. ¥ Adult 700, Children 400

SUNSHINE PLANETARIUM | 30

サンシャインプラネタリウム | D6

On the 10th floor of Sunshine City's World Import Mart, this planetarium offers not only a chance to study the stars, but a romantic experience with stories and music. The high-tech video and sound systems are computer controlled and of exceptional quality. The regular program changes with each season of the year. Also popular are the special program based on Greek mythology (from 5:30 pm. on weekdays) and the musical program (from 6 pm. on Saturdays).

3-1-3 Higashi-Ikebukuro, Toshima-ku ☎ 3989-3466 ⑤ Higashi-Ikebukuro Sta. ⏰ 11:00-17:30 (Sat. -18:00 Sun. & hol. 10:00-18:00) Ⓗ None ¥ Adult 720 Children 500

GOTO PLANETARIUM

NATIONAL MUSEUM OF WESTERN ART | 31

国立西洋美術館 | Kokuritsu Seiyo Bijutsukan | **D4**

NATIONAL MUSEUM OF WESTERN ART

Founded in 1959 around the 370-piece collection of businessman Kojiro Matsukata when the works he had collected while in Europe were returned by the French government after the end of World War II. The museum has since made additional acquisitions and the Rodin collection, including "Le Penseur" and "Les Bourgeois de Calais" in the garden, is one of the finest in the world. In addition to the permanent collection, special exhibitions of works borrowed from European and American museums are held three times a year. The main building was designed by French architect Le Corbusier. The new wing contains print, sketch and other specialized exhibit halls.

7-7 Ueno-koen, Taito-ku ☎ 3828-5131 S JR Ueno Sta. ⊙ 9:30-16:30 H Mon. (or the day after a Monday holiday). ¥ 360 (Ordinarily) Fees for special exhibits vary.

TOKYO METROPOLITAN TEIEN MUSEUM | 14

東京都庭園美術館 | Tokyo-to Teien Bijutsukan | **B3**

This handsome art deco building was constructed in 1933 to serve as the residence of Prince Asaka. After World War II, it was used as a reception hall but in consideration of the high artistic merit of the structure it was opened to the public as an art museum in 1983. It has no collection of its own but exhibitions of ornaments, arts and crafts which often recreate the sensibilities of the thirties are held five times a year. A sculpture by Zadkin stands in the garden *(Teien)*, treasured in itself as an oasis amid the concrete.

5-21-9 Shiroganedai, Minato-ku ☎ 3443-0201 JR Meguro Sta. ⊙ 10:00-17:30 H 2nd & 4th Wed. and during exhibit changes ¥ Varies with exhibit

TOKYO METROPOLITAN TEIEN MUSEUM

IDEMITSU MUSEUM OF ART | 13
出光美術館   Idemitsu Bijutsukan | E1

Established in 1966 to display the private collection of the founder of Idemitsu Kosan Co., Ltd. The ceramic collection is of particular note. In addition to old *Karatsu*, *Kutani* and *Imari* works from Japan, there are superb examples from all over Asia, Turkey and Egypt. The Sengai *Zen* painting collection is also known widely.

3-1-1 Marunouchi, Chiyoda-ku ☎ 3213-9402 [S] [JR] Yurakucho Sta. [S] Hibiya Sta. ⊙ 10:00-17:00 [H] Mon. and during exhibit changes [¥] 500

HARA MUSEUM OF CONTEMPORARY ART | 14
原美術館   Hara Bijutsukan | D5

The western-style building was erected in 1938 but did not become a museum until 1979. In addition to the sixty-odd piece permanent collection of modern masters such has Jackson Pollock, Andy Warhol and Yves Klein, special exhibitions of contemporary subjects such as pop art, computer graphics and video art are held regularly.

4-7-25 Kita-Shinagawa, Shinagawa-ku ☎ 3445-0651 Bus from [JR] Shinagawa Sta. ⊙ 11:00-17:00 (Wed.-20:00) [H] Mon. [¥] 700

ALTERNATIVE MUSEUM | 27
P3 オルタナティブミュージアム東京 | H4

The most common complaint among modern artists in Japan is probably that there is not enough space to fully appreciate their works. Not only are most galleries cramped, the ceilings are low. In answer to this need, a 250 sq.m gallery has been set up in the basement of Tochoji Temple, a *Sodo* sect, Buddhist temple, near Shinjuku Gyoen Garden. Built some four hundred years ago, the ceiling is 5 m high. Although the gallery has no permanent collection. A resource library and lectures are just some of the gallery's wide scope of activities.

4-34 Yotsuya, Shinjuku-ku ☎ 3353-6866 [S] Shinjukugyoen-mae Sta. ⊙ 13:00-18:00 [H] Mon. and between exhibitions [¥] Varies with exhibit

GOTO MUSEUM | —
五島美術館   Goto Bijutsukan | —

The collection of businessman Keita Goto. In addition to Japanese art objects such as tea ceremony utensils, picture scrolls, swords and sutras, Chinese ceramics and other Oriental antiques can be found in abundance. The "Tale of Genji Picture Scroll" and "Diary of Shikibu Murasaki Picture Scroll" have been designated National Treasures. Exhibits change seven times a year and one or two special exhibitions are held too. The museum covers some 20,000 sq. m. Stone Buddhas and stone lanterns dot the quiet garden. The building is constructed in a symmetrical architectural style called *Shindenzukuri* which was commonly used for the homes of the aristocracy during the Heian period (9-12 cent.). The museum also offers lectures and pottery classes.

3-9-25 Kaminoge, Setagaya-ku ☎ 3703-0661 [P] Tokyu-Oimachi Line Kaminoge Sta. ⊙ 9:30-16:30 [H] Mon. (or the day after a Monday holiday) and during exhibit changes. [¥] Varies with exhibit

NEZU INSTITUTE OF ART | 23

根津美術館   Nezu Bijutsukan | H5

A collection of some 7,000 works of far eastern art based around the private collection of businessman Kaichiro Nezu. The collection is quite diverse, including paintings, sculpture, textiles, and ceramics. Seventy-six pieces are Important Cultural Properties while the "Swallow and Flower Screen" is one of the seven National Treasures owned by the museum.

6-5-36 Minami-Aoyama, Minato-ku ☎ 3400-2536
[S] Omote-sando Sta. ⏰ 9:30-16:30 [H] Mon. [¥] Varies with exhibit

OTA MEMORIAL MUSEUM OF ART

HATAKEYAMA MEMORIAL HALL | 14

畠山記念館   Hatakeyama Kinenkan | C4

A must for anyone interested in the tea ceremony. The superb collection of utensils contains six National Treasures and thirty-three Important Cultural Properties. The tea ceremony garden and rooms provide a better understanding of the way of tea. The collection is that of engineer and businessman Issei Hatakeyama.

2-20-12 Shiroganedai, Minato-ku ☎ 3447-5787
[S] Takanawadai Sta. ⏰ April-September 10:30-16:30 / October-March 10:30-16:00 [H] Mon. and during exhibit changes [¥] 500

OTA MEMORIAL MUSEUM OF ART | 22

浮世絵太田記念美術館   Ukiyo-e Ota Kinen Bijutsukan | C5

This museum specializes in *ukiyo-e*. The collection contains some 10,000 wood block prints, 500 paintings and 900 painted fans by world-famous artists such as Hokusai Katsushika, Sharaku Toshusai, and Utamaro Kitagawa. It is a valuable resource for researchers on art and life in Japan. English explanations are provided.

1-10-10 Jingu-mae, Shibuya-ku ☎ 3403-0880 [JR] Harajuku Sta. [S] Meiji-jingu-mae Sta. ⏰ 10:30-17:00 [H] Mon. and the 24th to the end of the month [¥] 500(ordinarily) 800(special exhibits)

SEIJI TOGO MEMORIAL YASUDA KASAI MUSEUM OF ART | 26

安田火災東郷青児美術館   Yasuda-kasai Togo-Seiji Bijutsukan | C2

This museum is found on the 42nd floor of the super-skyscraper head office of the Yasuda Fire and Marine Insurance Co., Ltd. A prominent 20th century artist, western-style painter Seiji Togo's graceful works brim with his adoration of the female form. The museum was founded with 250 of Togo's works and 250 works by artists such as Ikuma Arishima, Saburo Miyamoto, Rodin and Picasso as well as Buddhist sculpture. More recently, Grandma Moses, Renoir, Tsuguji Fujita, and Ryusei Kishida works have been added. The most famous addition is the 1987 purchase of Van Gogh's "Sunflowers" for 5.3 billion yen. The exhibits of the permanent collection are changed two or three times a year.

1-26-1 Nishi-Shinjuku, Shinjuku-ku ☎ 3349-3081
[S] [JR] ShinjukuSta. ⏰ 9:30-16:30 [H] Mon. (open on Monday holidays) [¥] 500

SAGACHO EXHIBIT SPACE | 18
佐賀町エキジビットスペース | C6

Although at first glance this looks like nothing more than an old building, it survived the near destruction of Tokyo during World War II and has avoided the clutches of developers. Few structures in Tokyo predate this 1927 Art Deco Building. In the 26 sq. m space on the third floor, modern artists of the entire artistic spectrum hold short term exhibits. The exhibits are changed quickly to provide a forum for young artists.

1-8-13 Saga, Koto-ku ☎ 3630-3243 ◷ 11:00-18:00 Ⓢ Monzen-nakacho Sta. Ⓗ Mon. and during exhibit changes ¥ Free

SAGACHO EXHIBIT SPACE

GALLERY FACE | 22
ギャラリーフェイス | C4

This gallery is found in Harajuku, the haunt of young people. Exhibitions of pop art are changed every two weeks in the 150 sq.m gallery. The unique aspect of Gallery Face is that it contains a bar. The owners believe that art should be an integral part of our daily lives rather than isolated in museums.

2-32-5 Jingu-mae, Shibuya-ku ☎ 3401-0315 ⒿⓇ Harajuku Sta. ◷ 11:00-18:00 Ⓗ Mon. ¥ Free

TOKYO STATION GALLERY | 13
東京ステーションギャラリー | H2

Constructed in 1913, Tokyo Station is the gateway to Tokyo. The red brick Marunouchi side is one of the most well-known landmarks in Tokyo and controversy has arisen as to its preservation. The gallery opened in a corner of this building in 1988 offers two-month exhibitions four or five times a year. There are four exhibit rooms and although small, the gallery strives to offer quality, showing unique exhibits on foreign culture, history, art and architecture.

Tokyo Terminal Building ☎ 3212-2485 Ⓢ ⒿⓇ Tokyo Sta. ◷ 10:00-20:00 Ⓗ Mon. and during exhibit changes ¥ Varies with exhibit

TOKYO STATION GALLERY

HILLSIDE GALLERY | 25
ヒルサイドギャラリー | G6

Found in a corner of Hillside Terrace in Daikanyama. Every year twenty one-man shows by promising young modern artists are held here. About 20% are shows by foreign artists. Prints and lithographs are sold at the Art Front Gallery across the street.

29-18-A-1 Sarugaku-cho, Shibuya-ku ☎ 3476-4683 Ⓟ Tokyu-Toyoko Line Daikanyama Sta. ◷ 11:00-19:00 Ⓗ Mon. ¥ Free

TOKYO NATIONAL MUSEUM | 31

東京国立博物館 Tokyo Kokuritsu Hakubutsukan | **D3**

The largest art museum in Japan. The collection is displayed in four buildings. Archaeological relics can be found in the Hyokei Building, itself an Important Cultural Property constructed in the late 19th century. The Main Hall contains textiles, armaments, lacquer, books and other Japanese artworks. The Horyuji Temple Treasure House contains cultural relics from the 7th and 8th centuries while the Asian Hall contains objects from all over Asia and Egypt. It would take days to view the entire 88,000 object collection. A walk through the garden, complimented by a tea house and stone statues, is a pleasant way to relax after viewing the art.

Ueno-Koen, Taito-ku ☎ 3822-1111 [S] [JR] Ueno Sta. ◷ 9:00-16:00 [H] Mon. [¥] 360

MUSEUM OF MARITIME SCIENCE | 15

船の科学館　　Fune no Kagakukan | **H6**

The building was constructed to resemble a six-ton passenger ship on land reclaimed from Tokyo Bay. Exhibits include the main armaments from the Antarctic observation vessel "Soya" and warship "Mutsu", deep sea submarine PC-18 and other objects related to marine development, the navy and shipbuilding. The 70 m tall observation tower offers a panoramic view of the city.

3-1 Higashi-Yashio, Shinagawa-ku ☎ 3528-1111 [JR] Shinagawa Sta. ◷ 10:00-16:30 [H] None [¥] 500

THE NATIONAL SCIENCE MUSEUM | 31

国立科学博物館 Kokuritsu Kagaku Hakubutsukan | **D4**

The only science museum in Japan, the staff researches and collects data on natural history and science as well as displays it. The Main Building shows the inception and development of the human race. Other halls include Natural History, Aero-Space, Scientific Technology and Investigation. English explanations are provided.

7-20 Ueno-Koen, Taito-ku ☎ 3822-0111 [JR] Ueno Sta. ◷ 9:00-16:00 [H] Mon. [¥] 360

THE NATIONAL SCIENCE MUSEUM

TRANSPORTATION MUSEUM | 29

交通博物館　　Kotsu Hakubutsukan | **H4**

Vehicles are fascinating to people of all ages. Both model and real trains, boats, airplanes and every other kind of conveyance are on display in this museum. Palanquins and rickshaws are found in the "Man-powered Transportation" exhibit while "Transportation of Tomorrow" contains a linear motor car. Another attraction is the simulator for engineering the *Shinkansen*.

1-25 Kandasuda-cho, Chiyoda-ku ☎ 3251-8481 [S] [JR] Akihabara Sta. ◷ 9:30-16:30 [H] Mon. (or the day after a Monday holiday) [¥] 260

KITE MUSEUM	18
凧の博物館　　Tako no Hakubutsukan	D5

A display of the personal collection of the owner of the famous restaurant "Taimeiken". Japanese kites with *ukiyo-e*, Korean, Chinese, Thai, Malaysian, Italian and French kites — a total of 4,000. The theme-based exhibits are changed each month.
1-12-10 Nihonbashi, Chuo-ku ☎ 3271-2465 [S] Nihonbashi Sta. ⏱ 11:00-17:00 [H] Sun. and holidays [¥] 200

THE SHITAMACHI MUSEUM	31
下町風俗資料館 Shitamachi Fuzoku Shiryokan	C5

The Ueno area was once the downtown, or *shitamachi* of Tokyo. It played a central part in the lives of city residents. This museum seeks to recreate this atmosphere. The collection of some 56,000 items of furniture, clothing and daily sundries is made up of donations from local residents. English explanations are provided.
2-1 Ueno-koen, Taito-ku ☎ 3823-7451 [S] [JR] Ueno Sta. ⏱ 9:00-16:30 [H] Mon. (the day after a Monday holiday) [¥] 200

THE JAPAN FOLK CRAFTS MUSEUM	–
日本民芸館　　Nippon Mingeikan	–

Mingei is a word created by the founder of this museum, Soetsu Yanagi, to mean the objects used in traditional daily life. Pottery and porcelain, woven and dyed goods, woodwork, lacquer ware, paintings metalwork, stonework, bamboo ware, paper products, sculptures and paintings — everything is characterized by the primitive beauty of folk art.
4-3-33 Komaba, Meguro-ku ☎ 3467-4527 [P] Inokashira Line Komaba Todai-mae Sta. ⏱ 10:00-16:00 [H] Mon. [¥] 700

SUMO MUSEUM	–
相撲博物館　　Sumo Hakubutsukan	–

Data on the national sport, *sumo*, is collected and preserved here. The collection includes 3,700 colored wood block prints by artists such as Sharaku and Utamaro, 3,600 *banzuke* (programs) from the Edo period, *sumo* dolls, loincloths, umpire's fans and personal belongings of champions. Not to be missed by anyone with even the slightest interest in *sumo*. Exhibits are changed every two months.
1-3-28 Yokoami, Sumida-ku ☎ 3622-0366 [JR] Ryogoku Sta. ⏱ 9:30-16:30 [H] Sat., Sun., hol. [¥] Free

THE SHITAMACHI MUSEUM

FUKAGAWA EDO MUSEUM	–
深川江戸資料館 Fukagawa Edo Shiryokan	–

The actual streets of Tokyo some 150 years ago, when it was still called Edo, have been recreated like a movie set. Contemporary sundries and furniture are on display. Everything can be held and examined. Even the rise and setting of the sun are portrayed with lights (about 20 min.).
1-3-28 Shirakawa, Koto-ku ☎ 3630-8625 [S] Monzen-nakacho Sta. ⏱ 10:00-17:00 [H] None [¥] 300

TOBACCO AND SALT MUSEUM

	24
たばこと塩の博物館	D2

This unusual museum has taken two every day items, tobacco and salt as its theme. The 2nd floor mezzanine exhibits describe tobacco's indigenous environment and how it spread throughout the world in addition to cigarette packages and smoking gear from around the world. The 2nd floor is "Tobacco of Japan" and portrays the culture of tobacco in Japan since it arrived in the 16th century. The 3rd floor contains "Salt of Japan, Salt of the Earth" and uses dioramas and images to describe the history of salt and salt making in Japan.

1-16-8 Jinnan, Shibuya-ku ☎ 3476-2041 [S] [JR] Shibuya Sta. 🕙 10:00-17:30 [H] Mon. [¥] 100

TOBACCO AND SALT MUSEUM

TEPCO ELECTRIC ENERGY MUSEUM

	24
電力館 Denryoku-kan	D3

Abundant diagrams and models familiarize the consumer with how electricity is made, transmitted and used. Some highlights included an explanation of the transmission network through magic vision, an actual-size model of underground cables and a simulation of hydroelectric power produced by water mill.

1-12-10 Jinnan, Shibuya-ku ☎ 3477-1191 [S] [JR] Shibuya Sta. 🕙 10:30-18:30 [H] Wed. (the day after a Wednesday holiday) [¥] Free

NHK TENJI PLAZA

	24
NHK展示プラザ	A2

See drama sets, sound effects and program recording and all the other behind-the-scenes activities that go into making the TV programs we enjoy. Popular exhibitions (*tenji*) include testing of state-of-the-art broadcasting technology like Hi-Vision and the satellite broadcasting system.

2-2-1 Jinnan, Shibuya-ku ☎ 3485-8034 [JR] Harajuku Sta. [S] Meiji-jingu-mae Sta. 🕙 10:00-16:30 (Apr.-Sep.-17:30) [H] 2nd or 4th Mon. [¥] Free

PENTAX GALLERY

	16
ペンタックスギャラリー	A5

Opened in 1967, just as the rest of the world was becoming aware of the quality of Japanese cameras. It houses a collection of vintage cameras, projectors, enlargers and other relics totaling 4,000 that tell the history of photography.

3-21-20 Nishi-Azabu, Minato-ku, ☎ 3401-2186 [S] Roppongi Sta. 🕙 10:00-17:30 [H] Sun., hol., August [¥] Free

SMALL MUSEUM OF MUSICAL BOXES

	30
オルゴール館 Orugoru-kan	B6

Music boxes were invented by a watchmaker in late eighteenth century Switzerland. A hundred and fifty fine examples can be found in this little museum. The first floor contains the Introductory section where fine examples from Switzerland, Germany, America and other countries can be heard. The third and fourth floor contain the Applied Knowledge section. The finest examples of the art are collected here.

3-25-14 Mejirodai, Bunkyo-ku ☎ 3941-0008 [S] Gokokuji Sta. 🕙 Performances at 13:30 and 15:00. [H] Sun. and hol. [¥] 500

WORLD MAGAZINE GALLERY	12
ワールドマガジンギャラリー	C5

A magazine library on the premises of Magazine House, publisher of many popular magazines. Some 1,200 magazines from 50 countries, their back numbers (3 to 6 mo. previous), and newspapers can be read freely. The aisles are filled with tourists and expatriates looking for news from home. Mail-order catalogs are another useful feature. None of the magazines are loaned but the stacks are open and assistance is available in English, Italian, and French.
3-13-10 Ginza, Chuo-ku ☎ 3545-7227 |S| Higashi-Ginza Sta. ⏱ 10:00-19:00 |H| Sun. and hol. |¥| Free

WORLD MAGAZINE GALLERY

MEIYU INTERNATIONAL LIBRARY	12
明裕国際図書館 Meiyu Kokusai Toshokan	C4

Of the some 6,000 books in the collection on photography, design, art and advertising, about 3/4 are from other countries. Back numbers of photography magazines such as Asahi Camera, Mainichi Camera, Photo (France), and Modern Photography (U.S.A.) can be found in abundance. Bring ID.
4-8-8 Ginza, Chuo-ku ☎ 3561-1189 |S| Ginza Sta. ⏱ 11:00-17:00 |H| Sat., Sun. and hol. |¥| Free

JETRO LIBRARY AND INFORMATION SERVICE	17
ジェトロライヴラリー	G4

A reference library containing 60,000 books, 7,500 compilations of statistics, 2,500 company directories, custom charge charts for 120 countries, 400 newspapers and magazines from Europe, America, Asia and Africa, telephone books from the major cities of the world and mail-order catalogs. No loans.
2-2-5 Toranomon, Minato-ku ☎ 3582-1775 |S| Toranomon Sta. ⏱ 9:30-16:30 |H| Sat., Sun., hol. 3rd Tue. |¥| Free

TOKYO METROPOLITAN CENTRAL LIBRARY

TOKYO METROPOLITAN CENTRAL LIBRARY	20
都立中央図書館 Toritsu Chuo Toshokan	D4

One of the three metropolitan libraries in Tokyo. Of the 1,170,160 volumes in the collection (as of March 31, 1990), some 70,000 are foreign books and magazines. A wide variety of newspapers are available too. Numerous white papers and government publications are stored here. No loans.
5-7-13 Minami-Azabu, Minato-ku ☎ 3442-8451 |S| Hiro-o Sta. ⏱ 13:00-20:00 (Mon.), 9:30-20:00 (Tue.-Fri.), 9:30-17:00 (Sat., Sun. & hol.) |H| 1st Thur. 3rd Sun. |¥| Free

TOTO SUPER SPACE | 26
トート・スーパースペース | C2

A showroom on the water we use in our daily lives. New information on the bathroom and kitchen is presented in display spaces like "Kitchen Forum" and "Bathroom Avenue". As dull as it might seem, the appliances are displayed with artistic panache and even the toilets become artwork. Other features include the tile showroom Toilet Zone, the Life Design Boutique for sundries, Studio Theater with a 60 in. high-vision screen for introducing products and Project Plaza for events. You will discover a new perspective on everyday objects.

1-6-1 Nishi-Shinjuku, Shinjuku-ku ☎ 3345-1010 ⑤ JR Shinjuku Sta. ⊘ 10:00-18:00 Ⓗ None ¥ Free

TEPIA | 22
テピア | D1

An information showroom sponsored by the Machinery and Information Industries Promotion Foundation. Tepia Plaza on the 1st floor introduces machine information system technology. In the Library Zone on the 2nd floor, the latest AV equipment provides access to industrial data of all sorts. Examples include "Imported Food and Radiation" by Tokyo Electric Power Co., Inc. and "Japan, the Country of Photography" by Konica Corp. About 900 tapes on a variety of fascinating subjects are available for your perusal.

2-8-44 Kita-Aoyama, Minato-ku ☎ 5474-6111 ⑤ Gaien-mae Sta. ⊘ 10:00-18:00 (Wed. -19:00. Sat., Sun. & hol. -17:00) Ⓗ Mon. ¥ Free

HONDA WELCOME PLAZA | 23
ホンダウェルカムプラザ | G1

The newest Honda lines (both 2- and 4-wheel) are arrayed in full on an exhibit space covering about 1,000 sq. m. Filmed motor sports are projected on to a gigantic screen while the body sonic floor puts you where the action is. Other features include an F1 special exhibit space, F1 goods sales counter and Cafe Welcome.

2-1-1 Minami-Aoyama, Minato-ku ☎ 3423-4118 ⑤ Aoyama-Itchome Sta. ⊘ 9:30-18:30 (Sat., Sun., hol. 10:00-18:00) Ⓗ None ¥ Free

TOTO SUPER SPACE

LIFE SKETCH PLAZA | 14
松下電エライフスケッチプラザ | B3

A showroom for the latest equipment for living by Matsushita Electric Works, Ltd. Exhibits such as "Future Living Zone" and "Comfortable Living Experience Zone" on the first floor let you experience how electric appliances can make your life more comfortable. The second floor is a product showroom which includes 15,000 light fixtures. You'll be sure to find something that will improve your home.

4-8-2 Shiba, Minato-ku ☎ 3454-6111 ⑤ Mita Sta. ⊘ 10:00-18:00 Ⓗ None ¥ Free

NEC C&C PLAZA | 12
C＆Cプラザ | B1

The NEC Corporation showroom is designed around the theme of computers and communication. Sections on PC engine computer games and personal computers are just some of the things that will provide a full day's amusement for the computer buff.
2-2-3 Uchisaiwaicho, Chiyoda-ku ☎ 3595-0511 Ⓢ Uchisaiwaicho Sta. 🕐 10:00-18:00 Ⓗ Irregular ¥ Free

PIONEER SHOWROOM | 14
パイオニアショールーム | B4

The complete product line of audio equipment manufacturer Pioneer is on display. Not only can you test the stereos, but laser discs and car audio equipment as well. Feel the sound of *karaoke*, the musical accompaniment for singing so popular in Japan, in Body Sonic. If you're interested in audio equipment, you could easily spend half a day here.
1-4-1 Meguro, Meguro-ku ☎ 3495-9900 JR Meguro Sta. 🕐 10:30-18:50 Ⓗ None ¥ Free

TOKYO STOCK EXCHANGE | 18
東京証券取引所 Tokyo Shoken Torihikijo | C6

Kabuto-cho is to Tokyo what Wall Street is to New York or the City is to London. Look over the pandemonium of the Tokyo Stock Exchange through the glass on the second floor. The plaza contains a video explaining the mechanism of the stock exchange in Tokyo, a simulation game for stock trading and other interesting exhibits.
2-1 Nihonbashi Kabuto-cho, Chuo-ku ☎ 3666-0141 Ⓢ Kayabacho Sta. 🕐 9:00-16:00 Ⓗ Sat., Sun. & hol. ¥ Free

SONY BUILDING | 12
ソニービル | D3

Erected in 1966 to serve as a showroom for electrical appliance manufacturer Sony Corporation. The eight story building also contains showrooms of Toyota Motor Corporation, Fuji Xerox Co., Ltd., Japan Tobacco, Inc., a multi-purpose hall called Somido, restaurants and boutiques. The facade, fit with 2,300 brown pipes, is a local landmark where people often arrange to meet dates.
5-3-1 Ginza, Chuo-ku ☎ 3573-2371 Ⓢ Ginza Sta. 🕐 11:00-20:00 Ⓗ None ¥ Free

TOSHIBA GINZA SEVEN | 12
東芝銀座セブン | B7

A showroom packed with all the latest products from Toshiba Corp. You can try out everything from computer systems to kitchens. Especially popular are the AV sections. They contain 600 videos, 1,000 CD's and 600 LP's which can be sampled.
7-9-19 Ginza, Chuo-ku ☎ 3571-5971 Ⓢ Ginza Sta. 🕐 11:00-19:00 Ⓗ Wed., 2nd & 4th Tue. ¥ Free

TOKYO STOCK EXCHANGE

EXHIBIT SPACES

Tokyo is at the center of world economics. Domestic and foreign industry, trade promotion fairs, and many other kinds of exhibitions that reflect this are held every day and people come from far and wide to participate in them. However, as dense as the population is in Tokyo, there are few capacious spaces available. Here we will introduce two which were constructed for large-scale trade fairs. Parking and eating facilities are available. They transmit the latest technological, industrial and economic information throughout the country.

TOKYO INTERNATIONAL TRADE CENTER
東京国際貿易センター — —

In conjunction with the rapid economic growth of the day, this permanent trade fair grounds was constructed in 1959 on a broad area overlooking Tokyo Bay. Expansion has continued over the years so that now the center contains seven buildings, with exhibition space totaling 56,162 sq. m. More than a hundred trade fairs and exhibitions are held here annually and the total attendance surpasses 5 million. A schedule of events for the coming six months is published in the Trade Center News (in English), issued every January and July.

5-3-53 Harumi, Chuo-ku ☎ 3533-5311 Ⓢ Tsukiji Sta.

MAKUHARI MESSE

MAKUHARI MESSE
幕張メッセ — —

This convention center was erected in Makuhari New City Center, a part of Chiba Prefecture on the eastern edge of Tokyo, in October, 1989. The International Exhibition Hall contains 54,353 sq. m. of exhibit space and is the site for the Tokyo Motor Show and trade fairs for a wide variety of industries. In addition to the International Conference Hall which can seat 200 to 700, the Convention Hall which can house a party for 2,000 and smaller conference rooms are also provided. It is adjoined by the Makuhari Event Hall where all kinds of events are staged.

1-2 Nakase, Chiba-shi ☎ 0472-96-0001 ⒿⓇ Kaihin-Makuhari Sta.

TOKYO INTERNATIONAL TRADE CENTER

ACTIVITIES

Discover traditional Japan at Kabuki and Noh....
Modern-day Tokyo at its discos and clubs.

Tokyo, the Entertainment Capital

When it comes to entertainment, Tokyo lacks neither quality nor quantity. Among theaters, for example, while there remain only a limited number of venues specializing in traditional performances like *kabuki*, *rakugo*, and *noh*, the number of unique, contemporary theaters continues to grow every year. Recent years have also seen a new generation of movie theaters, more modern and comfortable than ever before. Prices vary depending on the program, but theatrical performances generally run from ¥2,000 to ¥10,000. Admission to first-run films is ¥1,600 or ¥1,700. Buying tickets in advance saves ¥200 - 300 from these prices. There are also special "Film Fan" days —— first day in the months of March, June, September, and December —— when all movie theaters offer half-price admission.

Music lovers have a choice of innumerable concerts, recitals, and other performances. Tokyo is a popular stop for many top international musicians, making it possible to see visiting foreign artists virtually any evening of the year. "Live houses" —— smaller, club-like venues —— are a Tokyo specialty, particularly in the Shinjuku and Roppongi areas. Many feature rock music for younger audiences, while others offer jazz in quieter surroundings, and yet others showcase traditional and ethnic types of music. Concert tickets range from about ¥2,000 to ¥10,000, while most live houses charge around ¥2,000. Performances generally begin around 6:30 pm.

Discos are a favorite gathering place of many young Tokyoites, and their numbers abound, especially in Roppongi. Here as elsewhere, though, the most popular and fashionable new spots tend to change rapidly. To find the best ones, avoid places that advertise by handing out discount coupons. Also be sure to dress appropriately: many of the most popular discos don't allow jeans or sneakers.

Admission is usually around ¥4,000.

One of the great attractions of Tokyo nightlife is the safety of the streets, no matter how late the hour. But do beware: some places charge exorbitant prices for even a single drink. When walking through areas like Shinjuku's Kabukicho, avoid any place where a tout or woman attempts to draw you in. Unless, of course, you're very adventurous ... and very wealthy.

Where to Buy Tickets

Obtaining tickets to plays and concerts can be as much of a headache in Tokyo as anywhere else. And the more popular the performance, the more effort it requires. For most ticket purchases, the most useful outlets are the ticket agencies found in major department stores. These include Playguide, Ticket Pia, and Ticket Saison. All handle tickets for various concerts and other musical performances, plays, sports events, films, etc. (but note that tickets for *rakugo* performances are sold only at the theaters). Tickets for more popular events have to be reserved by calling a number that appears in newspaper announcements. And for extremely popular shows, you may have to wait in line at a given place and time for numbers to be handed out, or send in a postcard for a lottery-type drawing. Complete information is available in Japanese-language entertainment magazines like "**Pia**", "**City Road**", and "**Tokyo Walker**". "**Tokyo Journal**", an English-language monthly, provides some of the same information in English. All these magazines are available at any larger bookstore. Another source of English-language information on films and plays is "**Tokyo Tour Companion**", published on the first and third Sunday of each month and distributed free of charge at major department stores and hotels.

NATIONAL THEATER OF JAPAN | 17

国立劇場　　　　Kokuritsu Gekijo | H1

Opened in 1966 to present the classical performing arts of Japan. The large hall (1,651 seats) features mainly *kabuki* performances. *Kabuki* appreciation classes are offered each June and July, with actors explaining and then demonstrating different themes in each session. The 630-seat small hall is the only venue in Japan offering a regular schedule (15 days in each of four months per year) of first-rate *bunraku* puppet theater at low admission fees. Headsets with English-language commentary are available.

4-1 Hayato-cho, Chiyoda-ku ☎ 3265-7411 Ⓢ Hanzomon Sta. ¥ 1,300-7,500 (Varies with performance)

KABUKIZA THEATER

KABUKIZA THEATER | 12

歌舞伎座　　　　　Kabuki-za | C4

Kabuki, Japan's performing art par excellence, began as a popular form of entertainment during the Edo period (1603-1867). Apart from the interest of the stories themselves, the beauty of the costumes make it well worth a visit. This theater, about a century old, preserves the atmosphere of an era when *Kabuki* was a favorite entertainment of the common man. The audience is free to watch entire performances, or take time out at the Japanese restaurant on the premises. Performance days vary each month. Headsets with English-language commentary are available. Tickets can be purchased at the Kabukiza ticket office, but reservations are advised.

4-12-15 Ginza, Chuo-ku ☎ 3541-3131 Ⓢ Higashi-Ginza Sta. ¥ Varies (standing space available)

NATIONAL THEATER OF JAPAN

SUEHIROTEI | 27

末広亭 | F3

Built in 1946, this small two-story wooden hall presents traditional Japanese story-telling and variety acts. Chairs and *tatami* mat areas seat a total of 325. Afternoon performances run from noon to 4:30 pm.; evening performances from 5:00 to 9: 30 pm. On weekdays you may stay for both sessions for the price of one. Young performers present a late-night show each Saturday from 10 pm.

3-6-12 Shinjuku, Shinjuku-ku ☎ 3351-2974 [S] Shinjuku-Sanchome Sta. [¥] 2,000

SUEHIROTEI

NATIONAL PERFORMING ARTS RESOURCE CENTER | 17

国立劇場演芸資料館Kokuritsu Gekijo Engei Shiryokan | H1

Houses a hall for *rakugo* story-telling, musical variety, and other popular traditional performing arts, as well as a library of recorded tapes of famous performers and books on related subjects. Performances, from 1:00 pm. to 4:30 pm., are the full-length classical versions. Particularly notable are performances by prominent storytellers on the fourth Saturday of each month.

4-1 Hayato-cho, Chiyoda-ku ☎ 3265-7411 [S] Hanzomon Sta. [¥] 1,500 (¥2,300 on Mon., 4th Sat.)

NATIONAL NOH THEATER | 22

国立能楽堂 Kokuritsu Nohgakudo | A1

Japan's only national theater for performance of noh, a traditional dramatic art that has changed little since taking shape in the 14th and 15th centuries. The theater presents its own performances about four days per month, with other *noh* groups appearing at other times. English programs are on sale in the lobby. Tickets may be purchased at the box office or at any Playguide ticket agency. Admission varies depending on the performance.

4-18-1 Sendagaya, Shibuya-ku ☎ 3423-1331 [JR] Sendagaya Sta.

SUZUMOTO ENGEIJO | 31

鈴本演芸場 | C5

Founded in 1857, this is Tokyo's oldest traditional variety hall. Now located inside a new building, it combines modern sound and lighting facilities with an authentic atmosphere of times past. Afternoon performances from 12:30 am. to 4:00 pm.; evening session from 5:20 to 8:30 pm. Seats 300.

2-7-12 Ueno, Taito-ku ☎ 3834-5906 [S] [JR] Ueno Sta. [¥] 2,000

ASAKUSA ENGEI HALL | 32

浅草演芸ホール | B2

In the years before World War II, this area of Asakusa was a lively center for variety halls, small play-houses and movie theaters. Today only this hall survives. Each day features a greater number of performers than at most other halls, and you are free to stay as long as you like, from the opening at 11:40 am. to the last curtain at 9:00 pm.

1-43-12 Asakusa, Taito-ku ☎ 3841-8126 [S] Asakusa Sta. [¥] 1,800

ACTIVITIES

PANASONIC GLOBE TOKYO	26
パナソニック グローブ座	E1

Tokyo's Globe theater is modelled on its namesake in London, home of Shakespeare and his company. There are a few differences, however. This one occupies part of a large condominium complex, and the decor is a stylish salmon pink and gray. It also features the latest in audio and lighting equipment. Performances — mostly of Shakespearean works, naturally — by both British and Japanese troupes. Seats about 700.

3-1-2 Hyakunin-cho, Shinjuku-ku ☎ 3360-1151 [S] [JR] Takadanobaba Sta. [JR] Shin-Okubo Sta.

PANASONIC GLOBE TOKYO

SPACE ZERO	26
スペースゼロ	C4

This unique theater incorporates the newest technology: a waterproof floor, for example, so that real water can be used for waterfalls. The technocube ceiling and the wall between the theater and foyer can be repositioned to change the proportions of the space. Performances include musicals, fashion shows, and plays.

2-12-10 Yoyogi, Shibuya-ku ☎ 3375-8741 [S] [JR] Shinjuku Sta.

TOKYO METROPOLITAN ART SPACE	30
東京芸術劇場 Tokyo Geijutsu Gekijo	B2

Completed in the autumn of 1990, this culture center forms part of the "Tokyo Renaissance" plan developed by the Office of Education of the Tokyo Metropolitan Government. The large hall, with 1,887 seats, allows large orchestral concerts, and includes a 126-stop French pipe organ. The 850-seat medium-size hall is designed for theater, opera, and dance. The two small halls each feature the very latest in stage facilities. Also of note are the exhibition hall and the spacious (1, 802 m²) entranceway. The result should prove to be a cultural oasis for both Tokyoites and visitors.

1-8-1 Nishi-Ikebukuro, Toshima-ku ☎ 5391-2111 [S] [JR] Ikebukuro Sta.

SPIRAL HALL	23
スパイラルホール	F6

Each year a new "artistic director" is named for this hall located on the third floor of this multi-purpose building. He or she then plans all the performances for the entire year. These range widely, from concerts and dance to theater and film, and often combine several different media. An exhibition, for example, might be accompanied by a related performance. The hall has already attracted considerable attention for its many new and experimental events.

5-6-23 Minami-Aoyama, Minato-ku ☎ 3498-5793 [S] Omote-sando Sta.

GINZA SAISON THEATRE | 13
銀座セゾン劇場 Ginza Sezon Gekijo | E4

Opened in 1987 specifically for theatrical performances. Food service is provided at the two-person box seats. The aim is to provide Tokyoites with a new type of entertainment facility. Performances, for example, begin later than the usual early hour, and the bar remains open after the show. The building also houses a movie theater and a hotel.
1-11 Ginza, Chuo-ku ☎ 3535-5151 Ⓢ Ginza-Itchome Sta.

THEATER TOPS | 27
シアタートップス | E2

With only 155 seats, this feels like a modern version of a traditional Japanese theater. Many of the plays, *rakugo* storytelling, talk shows, concerts, and other performances presented here take advantage of the proximity between stage and audience. Located near Shinjuku's Kabukicho entertainment district, the building also has a coffeehouse, a restaurant, and Western and Japanese-style bars.
3-20-8 Shinjuku, Shinjuku-ku ☎ 3350-9696 Ⓢ ⒿⓇ Shinjuku Sta.

HONDA THEATRE | –
本多劇場 Honda Gekijo | –

Since opening in 1982, this 386-seat theater has become a favorite venue for young drama groups. The stage is as large as the audience area, allowing the actors unusual freedom of movement. Several other theaters have since been built in the neighborhood, establishing Shimokitazawa as something of a theater community.
2-10-15 Kitazawa, Setagaya-ku ☎ 3468-0030 Ⓟ Inokashira Line Shimo-kitazawa Sta.

NISSAY THEATRE | 12
日生劇場 Nissei Gekijo | C1

Located amidst the Hibiya movie theater area. With 1,334 seats it is on the small side for a theater presenting major productions. Since its opening in 1963, Nissay has been used by the Toho and Shochiku entertainment companies and the Shiki theatrical troupe. Operas, musicals, plays, and other performances are generally presented for a run of about one month each.
1-1-1 Yuraku-cho, Chiyoda-ku ☎ 3503-3111 Ⓢ Hibiya Sta. Ⓢ ⒿⓇ Yurakucho Sta.

NISSAY THEATRE

IMPERIAL THEATER | 13
帝国劇場 Teikoku Gekijo | E1

Facing the Imperial Palace moat, this is Japan's oldest Western-style theater and showcase for many of its finest actors, actresses, and productions. About ten shows are presented per year, each running from one to two months. Summers are generally devoted to musicals; the rest of the year, to plays. 1,917 seats (some movable).
3-1-1 Marunouchi, Chiyoda-ku ☎ 3213-7221 Ⓢ Hibiya Sta. Ⓢ ⒿⓇ Yurakucho Sta.

Cinema Complexes

MULLION	12
マリオン	D2

Rising above JR Yurakucho and Marunouchi Line Ginza stations, the Mullion complex houses two department stores and Tokyo's largest single collection of movie theaters —— a total of seven, each usually showing a different film. On the 9th floor of the Seibu Department Store "A" Building are the Nichigeki Plaza, the Nichigeki Toho, and the Marunouchi Picadilly I and II; on the 11th floor is the Nihon Gekijo. On the 5th floor of the "B" Building is the Marunouchi Shochiku, and on the 7th floor, the Marunouchi Louvre. All feature currently popular Western and Japanese films.

2-5-1 Yuraku-cho, Chiyoda-ku ☎ 3574-1131 for Nichigeki Plaza, Toho, Nihon Gekijo ☎ 3201-2881 for Picadilly, Shochiku ☎ 3214-7761 for Louvre JR Yurakucho Sta.

MULLION

CHANTER	12
シャンテ	C1

This part of Hibiya is known for its movie theaters, and there are two in this building complex. Both Cine 1 and 2 have 226 seats and show mostly European films, particularly award winners and productions by new directors. Also screened here are a number of Asian films not presented anywhere else in Japan. Admission charges vary.

1-2-2 Yurakucho, Chiyoda-ku ☎ 3591-7251 Ⓢ Hibiya Sta.

KINECA OMORI	15
キネカ大森	D6

Located on the 5th floor of the Omori Seiyu Supermarket, Kineca 1, with 168 seats, shows first-run foreign and Japanese films, including somewhat lesser- known titles. Kineca 2, seating 82, specializes in films that have already been out for a while —— a good place to see films you missed the first time. Kineca 3, with just 52 seats, offers experimental and other films screened virtually nowhere else in Japan.

6-27-25 Minami-Ooi, Shinagawa-ku ☎ 3762-6000 JR Omori Sta.

IWANAMI HALL	28
岩波ホール	C5

Japan's film distributors tend to place profits before all else, with the result that they often fail to import outstanding but lower-profile films. Fortunately, Iwanami Hall has since 1974 been doing exactly that, providing Japanese audiences with first-run movies shown nowhere else. The hall is also home to a film lovers' organization known as "Equipe de Cinma." An invaluable resource for film buffs.

2-1 Kanda jinbo-cho, Chiyoda-ku ☎ 3262-5252 S
Jinbocho Sta.

CINE VIVANT	16
シネ・ヴィヴァン・六本木	B5

Roppongi's Wave sells a vast range of imported recordings, from classics to jazz, rock, and ethnic music, making it a cultural center of sorts for young people. Adding to the appeal is this small (194 seats) movie theater in the basement. Films are generally European and of high artistic calibre, presented without regard for fashion or fad.

6-2-27 Roppongi, Minato-ku ☎ 3403-6061 S
Roppongi Sta.

CINEMA TEN	16
俳優座シネマテン Haiyuza Cinema Ten	C5

The "Ten" in Cinema Ten refers to the time of the last show: the 10:00 pm. showtime is ideal for anyone working late or taking a leisurely dinner. The theater purchases and imports many films on its own, including Cannes festival winners. All are selected on the basis of artistic quality.

4-9-2 Roppongi, Minato-ku ☎ 3442-0438 S
Roppongi Sta.

CINEMA RISE SHIBUYA	24
シネマライズ渋谷	C3

A modern theater located at the top of the alley known as Spain Street in Shibuya. The interior walls are unadorned concrete and the lobby is decorated with artistic objects. Most films are minor European and American productions, and this is often the only place in Japan they are presented. The last showing each evening begins at 8:00 pm., slightly later than most Tokyo theaters.

13-17 Udagawa-cho, Shibuya-ku ☎ 3464-0052
S JR Shibuya Sta.

CINE VIVANT

IMAGE FORUM CINEMATHEK	27
イメージフォーラム	H5

This small (40 seats) theater specializes in independent productions and experimental films. Open only from Thursday to Sunday, it presents a different program each week. Several times a year it solicits and screens films by the public at large. Film fans can sign up for membership (free of charge) to receive program mailings and discount admission.

3-5 Yotsuya, Shinjuku-ku ☎ 3358-1983 S
Yotsuya-sanchome Sta.
🕐 Thur.- Sat. 17:00-19:00, Sun, hol. 13;00-15:00

SUNTORY HALL | 17

サントリーホール | **F4**

Occupying part of the Ark Hills complex, Suntory Hall is Japan's first hall designed and built specifically for full-scale concert performances. Completed in 1985, it seats 2,006 in stepped "vineyard" style around the stage. The Japan Philharmonic, Shinsei Nihon, Yomiuri Nippon, and Tokyo Metropolitan Symphony Orchestras all perform here on a regular basis. A number of other leading orchestras and artists from both Japan and abroad appear here as well.

1·13·1 Akasaka, Minato-ku ☎ 3505·1001 [S] Roppongi Sta.

SUNTORY HALL

TOKYO BAY NK HALL | –

東京ベイNKホール | **–**

A multi-purpose event space built on reclaimed land in Chiba Prefecture, neighboring Tokyo. Both audience seating and the stage area can be freely moved around the arena, and a large window directly in front of the stage affords a unique view of Tokyo Bay. Plays, concerts, and musicals are among the events held.

1·8 Maihama, Urayasu-shi, Chiba-ken ☎ 0473·55·7000 [JR] Maihama Sta.

CASALS HALL | 29

カザルスホール | **E4**

Named after the late Pablo Casals, the great Spanish cellist, this hall was designed specifically for chamber music. Using the same "shoebox" design as the Vienna Music Society Hall, it seats 511 in cozy comfort. The hall itself presents about 70 performances each year, and rents the hall out for a number of others.

1·6 Kanda-surugadai, Chiyoda-ku ☎ 3291·2525 [S] [JR] Ochanomizu Sta.

TSUDA HALL

TSUDA HALL | 22

津田ホール | **A1**

This 490-seat chamber music hall is renowned for the delicate sound provided by its acoustics. The hall organizes its own recitals, and its "Talk and Concert" events by Japanese and foreign musicians have been well received. Many symposium and other educational and cultural events are also held here.

1·18·24 Sendagaya, Shibuya-ku ☎ 3402·1851 [JR] Sendagaya Sta.

NHK HALL	24
NHK ホール	B1

NHK stands for Nippon Hoso Kyokai (Japan Broadcasting Corporation), the nation's sole public broadcaster. Its affiliated orchestra performs regularly at this hall, which is also used for concerts by other Japanese and foreign artists, as well as for recording of NHK radio and TV programs. With 3,677 seats, it is Japan's biggest concert hall. The stage is correspondingly large, allowing opera companies from abroad to perform with their full-size stage sets.
2-2-1 Jinnan, Shibuya-ku ☎ 3465-1751 JR Harajuku Sta. S Meiji-jingu-mae Sta.

NIPPON BUDOKAN	28
日本武道館	A6

Budokan means "martial arts hall" and indeed the Nippon Budokan was built in 1964 for judo competition at the Tokyo Olympics. Since that time this giant hall (seats 14,000) has been used not only for martial arts, but also for concerts and many other events. Features an impressive octagonal Japanese-style roof.
2-3 Kitanomaru-Koen, Chiyoda-ku. ☎ 3216-5100 S Takebashi Sta.

TOKYO DOME

SOUND COLOSSEUM MZA	15
MZA 有明	H5

This concert hall forms part of the huge MZA Ariake entertainment complex on Tokyo's fast-developing waterfront. Rock concerts and musicals are among the events held here, employing the hall's powerful lighting and sound systems. The MZA complex also contains a disco and various bars, cafes, and restaurants.
1-3-27 Ariake, Koto-ku ☎ 3529-5151 JR Shinagawa Sta.

SUN PLAZA HALL	–
中野サンプラザホール	–

Located within Nakano Sun Plaza, the large triangular building in front of Nakano Station. The hall is designed to be acoustically "dead," with the sound delivered to the audience via microphones and amplifiers. The effect is like that of a giant recording studio. Jazz, rock, and other concerts performed almost daily.
4-1-1 Nakano, Nakano-ku ☎ 3388-1151 S JR Nakano Sta.

TOKYO DOME (THE BIG EGG)	28
東京ドーム	A1

As both its names suggest, this stadium is covered by a huge dome. It serves as home to both the Yomiuri Giants of Japanese pro baseball's Central League, and the Nippon Ham Fighters of the Pacific League. It is also used for amateur baseball, American football, soccer, bicycle racing, concerts by Japanese and foreign acts, and even college entrance examinations. A sightseeing tour of the dome itself is offered.
1-3 Koraku, Bunkyo-ku ☎ 3811-2111 S Korakuen Sta. JR Suidobashi Sta.

ACTIVITIES

Multi-Purpose Facilities

TOKYU BUNKAMURA	24
東急文化村	**B4**

Opened in the autumn of 1988. Orchard Hall, designed to provide world-class sound, numbers among Japan's finest concert halls. With its "shoebox" design seating 2,150, it is also the largest. The acoustics have won rave reviews from audiences and performers alike. The smaller Theater Cocoon, with 747 seats, is used not only for theater but also musicals, operas, and fashion shows. The two venues operate Japan's first "in-house" performance arrangement, by means of an exclusive contract with the Tokyo Philharmonic Orchestra at Orchard Hall and with The On Theater Jiyu Gekijo at Theater Cocoon. Other facilities include the Cinema 1 and 2 theaters, specializing in art films; The Museum, with 830 sq. m of display area for various exhibitions; a recording studio, a gallery, a flower shop, a book store, and a cafe.

2-24-1 Dogenzaka, Shibuya-ku ☎ 3477-9111
⑤ JR Shibuya Sta.

NATIONAL CHILDREN'S CASTLE	25
こどもの城　　　Kodomo no Shiro	**H1**

Despite its name, there's plenty at the Children's Castle for adults too. The AV Library here stocks some 5, 200 video recordings of films, concerts, musicals, plays, and other performances. All are freely available for use for the single price of admission. There is also a pool, open to the public 10 am. - 5 pm. on Saturdays, Sundays, and holidays; admission: ¥310. Two theaters —— the Circle Theater and the Aoyama Theater —— present popular Japanese and foreign plays.

5-53-1 Jingu-mae, Shibuya-ku ☎ 3797-5666 ⑤
Omote-sando Sta.
🕐 13:00-17:30 (Sat. Sun. hol. from 10:00; 10:00-18:00 during summer months) ¥ 410 (entrance fee)

SUNSHINE CITY

SUNSHINE CITY	30
サンシャインシティ	**B2**

Just look for the 60-story white skyscraper towering over the east side of Ikebukuro. Rental offices fill most of the building, but the restaurants on the 58th and 59th floors and the observation deck on the 60th floor offer a superb view of the entire Kanto area, from Tokyo Bay and Mt. Fuji to Nikko and Mt. Tsukuba. The BUNKA KAIKAN (culture hall) houses a museum of ancient Oriental art and the Sunshine Theater, while the WORLD IMPORT MART includes an aquarium and a planetarium. "Sunshine City" refers to the entire complex (Sunshine 60, Bunka Kaikan, World Import Mart, and the adjacent 1, 166-room Sunshine Prince Hotel), which also incorporates a shopping center and a number of restaurants.

3-1 Higashi-Ikebukuro, Toshima-ku ☎ 3989-3331
⑤ JR Ikebukuro Sta.

Live Music Takes the Lead

One of the biggest changes in Japanese television and radio in recent years is the almost complete disappearance of the once-popular "hit parade" programs featuring various stars singing their newest songs.

Does this mean that popular music has fallen on hard times in Japan? Far from it. Sales of albums (now mostly CDs) by all kinds of popular artists are doing better than ever. The difference is that record companies find it harder these days to turn out ready-made "hits" — in other words, songs tailored for mass-market TV audiences. Increasingly, the new trends in pop music come from the innumerable amateur bands performing on their own at clubs, halls or outdoor venues.

BLUE NOTE TOKYO	23
ブルーノート東京	H6

The Tokyo franchise of New York's renowned Blue Note jazz club features the same blue decor as the original. Like the original too, it showcases some of the biggest names in jazz. Past acts have included Oscar Peterson, Herbie Hancock, and Sarah Vaughn. Note, however, that especially famous names command a charge of ¥10,000 or more. Be sure to telephone before you go: reservations are required.

5-13-3 Minami-Aoyama, Minato-ku ☎ 3407-5781 S Omote-sando Sta. ◯ 18:00-02:00 H Sun. ¥ 6,000-12,000 C JCB, VISA, MC, AMEX, others

CLUB QUATTRO

CLUB QUATTRO	24
クラブ・クアトロ	D4

This eye-catching club operates on the policy of presenting the very latest in music — even to the extent of starting its own "Quattro" recording label. Acts range from rock and jazz to reggae, samba, and black music, while audiences include everyone from teenagers to adults. The common link: an appreciation for the cutting edge in musical trends.

Quattro by Parco Bldg. 5F 32-13 Udagawa-cho, Shibuya-ku ☎3477-8750 S JR Shibuya Sta. ◯ 18:00-20:00 H None ¥ 2,000-5,500 C None

BLUE NOTE TOKYO

HOT COROCKET | 16
ホットコロッケ | D6

Rare is the reggae musician visiting Japan who doesn't perform at Hot Corocket, Tokyo's club for the reggae connoisseur. The dance floor lets you move to the beat, and the heavily foreign clientele creates a distinctly international mood.

Dai-ni Daisho Bldg. B1F 5-18-2 Roppongi, Minato-ku ☎ 3583-9409 ⓈRoppongi Sta. 🕐 19:00-3:00 Ⓗ None ¥ 3,000 ⒸJCB, DN, VISA, MC, AMEX, others

AFTER SIX | 16
アフター・シックス | C5

A quieter jazz club for intimate evenings around a piano. Most of the pianists come from the U.S., which may explain why about half the audience tend to be foreigners. Requests are welcome, and there will be no lack of favorite old standards like "As Time Goes By."

Zonan Bldg. B1F 3-13-8 Roppongi, Minato-ku ☎ 3405-7233 ⓈRoppongi Sta. 🕐 19:00-2:00 Ⓗ Sun. ¥ 2,500-5,000 ⒸJCB, DN, VISA, MC, AMEX, others

LOFT | 26
ロフト | D1

This club has provided grass-roots support for Japan's underground rock scene for some 14 years now. A number of bands got their start here before going on to bigger things. These days the orientation is toward new wave and punk, performed energetically. Particularly popular among junior high and high school students.

Dai-ni Mizota Bldg. B1F 7-5-10 Nishi-Shinjuku, Shinjuku-ku ☎ 3365-0698 Ⓟ Seibu-Shinjuku Line Seibu-Shinjuku Sta. 🕐 19:00-22:00 (Sat., Sun. & hol. 14:00-16:00) Ⓗ None ¥ 1,400-3,000 Ⓒ None

CAY | 23
カイ | G6

Where else in Tokyo can you enjoy live music while dining on authentic Thai food served by waiters and waitresses dressed in Thai costumes? Reggae and samba performances each Friday and Saturday night. The tropical-inspired interior and unique cocktails add to the enjoyment.

Spiral bldg. B1F 5-6-23 Minami-Aoyama, Minato-ku ☎ 3498-5790 Ⓢ Omote-sando Sta. 🕐 18:30-1:00 Ⓗ Sun. ¥ 7,000- 10,000 (live band) /5,000-8,000(no band) ⒸJCB, DN, VISA, MC, AMEX, others.

PIT INN

PIT INN | 16
ピット・イン | D5

Sister establishment of Shinjuku's renowned Pit Inn jazz club. Compared to its older sibling, the Roppongi club features a somewhat wider range of musical genres, ranging into fusion and rock. Big-name acts from abroad play here sometimes, but take note: tickets can sell out almost immediately.

Shimei Bldg. B1F 3-17-7 Roppongi, Minato-ku ☎ 3585-1061 ⓈRoppongi Sta. 🕐 18:30-23:00 Ⓗ None ¥ 2,500 Ⓒ None

J-POP

J-POP	24
ジェイ・ポップ	D4

Most *karaoke* sing-along bars tend toward traditional *enka* ballads. But not J-PoP, where you can sing some 400 favorite hits in a state-of-the-art setting. Get up on the stage here, amid laser beams, smoke machines and flashing mirror balls, and you too will feel like a rock star. And if that works up an appetite, the menu offers some 40 different dishes, mostly in the ¥800-1,000 range. Table charge: ¥1,500.

30-7 Udagawa-cho, Shibuya-ku ☎ 3464-4411 [S] [JR] Shibuya Sta. ⊙ 18:00-4:00 [H] Sun., hol. [¥] ★★ [C] JCB, DN, VISA, AMEX, UC

KENTOS	16
ケントス	C5

More of a dancing spot than a sit-down club, Kentos offers live — and lively — American pop music. From the decor to the match boxes to the music itself, the theme is "oldies", and fans of vintage rock will feel right at home. The band plays six sets of about one hour each, beginning at 7:30 pm. nightly.

Dai-ni Reine Bldg. B1F 5-3-1 Roppongi, Minato-ku ☎ 3401-5755 [S] Roppongi Sta. ⊙ 18:00-02:30 [H] None [¥] 1,300 [C] JCB, DN, VISA, MC, AMEX, others.

NISSIN POWER STATION	27
日清パワーステーション	G2

Located in the basement of "Foodeum," a large, stylish building that recently appeared in Shinjuku. In what might be described as a rock lounge-restaurant format, you can sit and dine while watching the band on a stage below. Age 20 and over only.

Foodeum B1F 6-28-1 Shinjuku, Shinjuku-ku ☎ 3205-5270 [S] Shinjuku-Sanchome Sta. ⊙ 17:30-22:30 [H] None [¥] Varies with players [C] None

J-POP

CAVERN CLUB	16
キャバーンクラブ	C5

The ultimate place for Beatles fanatics, whether Japanese or foreign, and filled with them every night. The band looks and sounds like the Fab Four, and even takes requests (Beatles numbers only, of course) on Tuesdays, Thursdays, and Saturdays. Supposedly Liverpool-inspired food is offered, with emphasis on seafood. The six sets nightly of about one hour each begin at 7:30 pm.

Saito Bldg. 1F 5-3-2 Roppongi, Minato-ku ☎ 3405-5207 [S] Roppongi Sta. ⊙ 18:00-2:30 [H] None [¥] 1,300 [C] JCB, DN, VISA, MC, AMEX, others.

CROCODILE	25
クロコダイル	E1

This could well be Tokyo's definitive live music house. It is certainly a favorite with the musicians who play there, largely because of the easy-going atmosphere. Any and all types of music are represented. In fact you can be assured of a reasonably good time no matter who is playing: just drop by any night.

New Sekiguchi Bldg. B1F 6-18-8 Jingumae, Shibuya-ku ☎ 3499-5205 [S] [JR] Shibuya Sta. ⊙ 18:00-2:00 [H] None [¥] 1,500-2,500 [C] None

SQUARE BUILDING | 16
スクエアビル | C5

SQUARE BUILDING

Tokyo's disco mecca is an entire building full of dancing spots. From the top down: on the 10th floor, The Circus (☎ 5474-0261) is well known for its black music beat. On the 8th floor, the glass-walled Nepenta (☎ 3470-0751) remains as popular among women as men, surviving for years in a town where discos come and go almost overnight. Bingo Bango Bongo (☎ 3479-5600) on the 7th floor opened in March 1990 and features an impressively artistic decor. The attraction at the 6th floor Venus (☎ 3470-0555) is a Bodysonic floor that moves with the music. Buzz (☎ 3470-6391) on the 5th floor is, as the name suggests, abuzz with activity nightly. On the 3rd floor is another famed survivor, Giza (☎ 3403-6538) with its unusual Egyptian and outer space motif. Finally on B1 is Java Jive (☎ 3478-0087), featuring in addition to disco dancing both a live reggae band and a dining area. Admission to any one of these is ¥4,000 for men and ¥3,000 for women (¥500 more at The Circus on weekends). Which one is best? The choice is up to you.

Square Bldg. 3-10-3 Roppongi, Minato-ku [S] Roppongi Sta. ⏱ 17:00-05:00 [H] None [C] JCB, DN, VISA, MC, AMEX

ROPPONGI PLAZA BUILDING | 16
六本木プラザビル | C5

Located in front of the Square Bldg., this second complex of dancing spots begins with the 6th floor Za Make-up (☎ 3479-1511; admission: ¥4,000 for men, ¥3,000 for women), which is equipped with a feature their women guests appreciate: a dressing room. On the 5th floor is Spats (☎ 3405-5700; admission ¥2,000 or ¥2,200 after 11 pm.; ¥2,200 or ¥2,500 after 11 pm. on weekends), presenting oldies by a live band in a high-energy atmosphere. The most popular place in the building is the 4th floor Vietti (☎ 3401-7478; admission ¥3,500 for men, ¥3,000 for women, ¥500 more on weekends), where women in particular seem to like the Italian modern interior. It also features a separate bar area, and the beer cocktails can be recommended. The entire building makes a good change of pace for disco-goers tiring of the Square Bldg.

Roppongi Plaza Bldg. 3-12-6 Roppongi, Minato-ku [S] Roppongi Sta. ⏱ 18:00-24:00 [H] None [C] JCB, DN, VISA, MC, AMEX

ROPPONGI PLAZA BUILDING

NITTAKU BUILDING | 16
| 日拓ビル | C5 |

This well known building offers live music on three floors. On the 3rd floor is the Oriental-style Cipango (☎ 3478-0039; admission ¥6,000, ¥500 more on weekends); on the 2nd floor, Lollipop (☎ 3478-0028; admission, ¥1,500-1,600); on the ground floor, Sensation (☎ 3479-7771; admission ¥1800). On the B2 level, you'll find Area (☎ 3479-3721; admission ¥4,500 for men, ¥4,000 for women, ¥500 more on weekends), a popular disco with a spacious seven-meter ceiling.
3-8-15 Roppongi, Minato-ku Ⓢ Roppongi Sta. 🕐 17:00-24:00 Ⓗ None Ⓒ JCB, DN, VISA, MC, AMEX

GOLD | 15
| ゴールド | F3 |

Among the new night spots recently appearing in the Shibaura warehouse district. This huge disco gives you a choice of four different floors, each with its own decor and music. A favorite with show business types and other celebrities.
3-1-6 Kaigan, Minato-ku ☎ 3453-3545 ⒿⓇ Hamamatsu-cho Sta. 🕐 18:00-24:00 Ⓗ None ¥ 4,000 (weekends 5,000) Ⓒ JCB, DN, VISA, MC, AMEX, others

S. I. JOE | 24
| エス・アイ・ジョー | D6 |

A popular Shibuya spot since its recent renovation. On Fridays and Saturdays, enjoy a dynamic show by Japan's leading dance teams. Or, any night after about 9 pm., a lively and slightly older than average (i.e., upper 20s and 30s) clientele.
Hotel P&A Plaza B1F 1-17-9 Dogenzaka, Shibuya-ku ☎ 3780-0720 Ⓢ ⒿⓇ Shibuya Sta. 🕐 18:00-24:00 Ⓗ None ¥ 4,000(men) 3,000(women) Ⓒ VISA MC, AMEX

NITTAKU BUILDING

GEOID | 16
| ジオイド | A6 |

This disco achieved a certain notoriety when it became Japan's first to offer a ¥10 million membership. The interior design was inspired by views of earth from outer space, which together with the state-of-the-art Italian lighting system creates a uniquely luxurious, mysterious mood.
3-5-5 Nishi-Azabu, Minato-ku ☎ 3479-8161 Ⓢ Roppongi Sta. 🕐 18:00-24:00 Ⓗ None ¥ 5,000(men) 4,000(women) (weekends +¥500) Ⓒ JCB, DN, VISA, MC, AMEX, others.

RONDE CLUB | 17
| ロンドクラブ | F2 |

The decor here is anything but the chic minimalism now in vogue: every corner of the place is covered in gold. The effect looks like something out of Europe's Middle Ages. The music too goes against the fashion for loudness, remaining moderate enough for conversation. A good choice for a relaxed, leisurely drink.
Pen Japan Bldg. B1F 3-8-17 Akasaka, Minato-ku ☎ 3589-6707 Ⓢ Akasaka-mitsuke Sta. 🕐 17:00-24:00 Ⓗ None ¥ 5,000(men) 4,000(women) Ⓒ JCB, DN, VISA, MC, AMEX, others.

ACTIVITIES

ABECHAN

KOKUCHO NO MIZUUMI | 27
黒鳥の湖 | F2

The emphasis at this transvestite cabaret is on humor, and the hilarious shows here attract a lively young crowd, including many women. Three acts per night: 8 pm., 10:30 pm., and 1 am. The shows change every three months. It's affordable too: from ¥3,000 per person.

2-25-2 Kabuki-cho, Shinjuku-ku ☎ 3205-0128 S JR Shinjuku Sta. ◷ 18:00-2:00 H Sun. ¥ ★★ C JCB, DN, VISA, MC, AMEX, others

CLUB MAIKO | 21
クラブ・マイコ | B3

As the name suggests, Club Maiko features performances by traditional *maiko* dancing girls. The dancers circulate among the tables during the breaks, talking with the customers. And they're happy to have their pictures taken with you (for ¥1,000 per shot) — just ask your waiter or waitress.

Aster Plaza Bldg. 4F 7-7-6 Ginza, Chuo-ku ☎ 3574-7745 S Ginza Sta. S JR Shinbashi Sta. ◷ 18:00-24:00 H None ¥ 12,000 C JCB, DN, VISA, MC, AMEX

ABECHAN | 27
アベチャン | F2

Tokyo doesn't lack for transvestite song-and-dance revues, but few match the elegance of Abechan. Shows (at 11:30 pm. and 1:30 am.) feature a troupe of about 20 beautifully costumed dancers in a disco-like mirrored decor. Be prepared to spend about ¥15,000 per person.

2-29-8 Kabuki-cho, Shinjuku-ku ☎ 3207-3567 S JR Shinjuku Sta. ◷ 21:00-4:00 H Sun., hol. ¥ ★★★★ C JCB, DN, VISA, MC, AMEX, others

CLUB MAIKO

EATING
AND
DRINKING

From Japanese cuisine
to French, Mexican or Thai....
A gourmet's-eye view of Japan's capital.

Gourmet Tokyo

Tokyo feeds more than 10 million residents, to say nothing of the many more daily commuters from outside the city and tourists from both Japan and abroad. It does this at eating and drinking shops of countless number and staggering variety. Naturally there is Japanese food, but there is also Chinese, French, Italian, Indian, German. . .in fact, most anything. Virtually every country to have an embassy in Tokyo seems to have its cuisine represented as well. If cost isn't an object, you can find almost any food from anywhere in the world in Tokyo, and usually of high quality.   Of the areas where bars and restaurants congregate, Shinjuku and Ikebukuro feature relatively inexpensive places. Shibuya caters to a young clientele, as do Aoyama and Roppongi but on a more upmarket level. Akasaka and Ginza are home to many top-quality Japanese and French restaurants. For Japanese food served in a traditional atmosphere, you need look no further than the old downtown area around Asakusa. This book by necessity focuses on these main areas, but of course there are many good places elsewhere, and we have tried to include as many as possible.

Visiting a Japanese Restaurant

Interested in trying the famous foods of Japan? Dishes like *sushi*, *tempura*, *shabu-shabu*, and *sukiyaki*? Well, the first thing you should realize is that these are relatively high-priced foods. And making it worse is that many restaurants in Japan, unlike those in the West, show no menu outside, making it hard to guess how much a meal will cost. So if you want to visit a Japanese restaurant of the better class, first ask a knowledgeable friend, or use a listing from these pages.

Naturally, Tokyo also has its share of excellent, low-cost restaurants, and we recommend a number of them in this book as well. Upon sitting down at most restaurants in Japan, you'll first receive a glass of water or green tea. There is no charge for this, and you should feel free to ask for refills. Ordering can be as simple as asking for the specialty of the house. In a *soba* restaurant, for example, you can simply say "One *soba*" ; in a spaghetti restaurant, "A bowl of spaghetti." Of course usually you'll have more of a choice, allowing you to order whatever you like. How about tipping? Unlike many other countries, Japan has no custom of tipping at restaurants. Just pay the amount shown on the bill.

Getting What You Want

When it comes time to choosing food or drink at a restaurant, the most important immediate factor will be how much English or other language the staff speaks. Of course this is true of other situations in Japan as well, but in a restaurant it can mean the difference between getting what you want or going hungry. In general, any restaurant listed in this book will have staff who can speak either English or else the language of the cuisine represented. They will also have a menu in the language of their cuisine. The problem, obviously, is at Japanese restaurants. Unfortunately we found few where the waiters and waitresses speak English with any real fluency. But many do have an English menu, and most told us that their foreign customers have no particular problems. Note that all of the restaurants listed here are popular places. This means that they will be crowded, especially on weekends. If a restaurant requires a reservation, we say so. Even if they don't, it's never a bad idea to call and tell them you're coming. (Exceptions are simple restaurants like *soba* and *ramen* shops or cake shops and cafes.)

KYUBEI	12
久兵衛	B2

This high-class restaurant is famed even in Ginza. The lunch set menu (10 *nigirizushi* [rice balls with fish on top], 1 *makizushi* [rice and fish rolled in seaweed] and *miso* [fermented bean paste] soup) is ¥6,000. The dinner set menu (almost the same as lunch) is ¥7,500. Ordering a la carte will run about ¥15,000 a person but it is well worth the price. There is a branch in the Hotel Okura.

8-5-23 Ginza, Chuo-ku ☎ 3571-6523 S JR Shinbashi Sta. ⏰ 11:30-14:00, 17:00-22:00 H Sun. and hol. ¥★★★★ C JCB, DN, VISA, MC, AMEX, others

KYUBEI

YOTSUYA-MATOIZUSHI	27
四谷纏鮨	H5

The ingredients here are nothing if not fresh. Everything is done to perfection. Set menus run ¥1,800-2,500 (7 *nigirizushi* and 1 *norimaki*). Ordering a la carte won't come cheap but the cook will adjust to your budget.

1-24 Yotsuya, Shinjuku-ku ☎ 3357-8957 S JR Yotsuya Sta. ⏰ 17:00-01:00 H Tue ¥★★★ C JCB, VISA, AMEX

SUSHISEI

NAKATA	12
なか田	C3

Ginza is full of *sushi* bars but this pre-World War II example has enjoyed steady popularity. Frozen fish is never used and traditional methods are stubbornly preserved. The cherished original wooden structure is undergoing renovation so business continues as usual at this temporary shop. A set menu of *nigirizushi* or *chirashi zushi* (Garnished sushi) is ¥3,300. There is a branch in the Imperial Hotel.

Chiyoda Trading Bldg. 6-7-19 Ginza, Chuo-ku ☎ 3571-0053 S Ginza Sta. ⏰ 12:00-21:30 H Sun. ¥★★★★ C VISA, MC, AMEX

TSUKIJI-TAMAZUSHI

HOW TO EAT SUSHI CHEAPLY

Sushi is one of the more expensive kinds of Japanese food but there are some places that trade on low prices. Genroku zushi and similar chains have a conveyer belt on which little plates of different kinds of *sushi* move by your counter seat. Just take what ever kind of *sushi* catches your fancy. Usually two pieces are contained on each plate and cost ¥100-150. Your check is computed by counting the stack of plates in front of you. There are also inexpensive chains like Kozozushi and Kozenizushi but they only offer take-out.

SUSHISEI (Main Shop)	12
寿司清	B6

Located right next to the Tsukiji Fish Market since 1887. The location assures a wide variety of the freshest ingredients. At only ¥100 to ¥300 per piece, you can freely sample any of the more than thirty types of *sushi*. Its popularity among nearby office workers means there is almost always a long line out front. Be prepared to wait.
4-13-9 Tsukiji, Chuo-ku ☎ 3541-7720 [S] Tsukiji Sta. ⏰ 1F 08:00-13:00, 17:00-19:30/2F 10:00-14:00, 17:00-21:30 [H] Sun. and hol. ¥★★ [C] None

TSUKIJI-TAMAZUSHI (Main Shop)	12
築地玉寿司	D6

Fresh, tasty *sushi* at a reasonable price. In addition to the traditional types of *sushi*, the menu includes Tamazushi originals like *Yofu* (western) *maki* — fish rolled with red-leaf lettuce and tartar sauce. Lunch is ¥900 and the dinner sets start from ¥1,500. Even on Sunday the counter is packed with businessmen. Reservations are necessary for private rooms.
1-9-4 Tsukiji, Chuo-ku ☎ 3541-1917 [S] Tsukiji Sta. ⏰ 11:00-22:00 [H] None ¥★★ [C] JCB,DN, VISA, MC, AMEX, others

TSURUHACHI	鶴八	2-4 Kanda Jinbo-cho, Chiyoda-ku	☎3262-0665	**28·C5**
YOSHINOZUSI	吉野鮨	2-21 Kanda Jinbo-cho, Chiyoda-ku	☎3261-2324	**28·C5**
SUSHIEI	すし栄	7-13-2 Ginza, Chuo-ku	☎3541-5055	**12·B4**
SUSHIYOSHI	寿司好	Honshu Bldg. 5-12-8, Ginza, Chuo-ku	☎3541-0329	**12·C4**
EDOGIN(Main Shop)	江戸銀	4-5-1 Tsukiji, Chuo-ku	☎3543-4401	**12.B5**
KIZUSHI	㐂寿司	2-7-13 Nihonbashi Ningyo-cho, Chuo-ku	☎3666-1682	**19·F6**
SUSHIKOMA	鮨駒	Naritaya Bldg. 3-14-3 Akasaka, Minato-ku	☎3585-1238	**17·F2**
OTSUNAZUSHI	おつな寿司	Hotel IBIS 1F, 7-14-4 Roppongi, Minato-ku	☎3401-9953	**16·C5**

ASAKUSA-IMAHAN	32
浅草今半	B2

The three-story building of this immense restaurant faces Kokusai-dori street in once bustling Asakusa. Founded in 1896, it has long been a favorite place to dine out among Tokyo residents. The *sukiyaki*, highly seasoned the way Tokyoites like it, and *shabu shabu* with special sauces are both made from extra-high quality Omi beef. The *sukiyaki* and *shabu shabu*·courses include an appetizer, rice (*udon* noodles for *shabu shabu*), *miso* soup and dessert and start at ¥6,000. For lunch there are ¥1,500 and ¥3,000 *sukiyaki* sets as well as ¥1,000 *gyudon* [beef on rice]. The private rooms containing *horigotatsu* (tables with wells underneath) for those of you not used to sitting on the floor and foreign visitors are presented with a special gift. It is better to make reservations.

3-1-12 Nishi-Asakusa, Taito-ku ☎ 3841-1114 S Tawaramachi Sta., Asakusa Sta. ◷ 11:30-22:00 H 1st and 3rd Tue. ¥★★★ C JCB, DN, VISA, MC, AMEX, others

SHINHEIKE	30
新平家	C2

Enjoy both *sukiyaki* and *shabu shabu* at this Ikebukuro restaurant. The famed Matsuzaka beef can be sampled at a comparatively reasonable price. A course menu containing both *sukiyaki* and *shabu shabu* starts at ¥6,000. *Kaiseki* courses start at ¥8,000

Romance Bldg. 1-36-8 Nishi-Ikebukuro, Toshima-ku ☎ 3982-8194 S JR Ikebukuro Sta. ◷ 11:30-14:30, 17:00-23:00 (Sat. and Sun. 11:30-22:00) ¥ ★★★ C JCB, DN, VISA, MC, AMEX, others

KISOJI	12
木曽路	C3

Matsuzaka beef is the best beef in Japan and nothing can compare to *shabu shabu* with marbled slices of it eaten in this quiet folk interior. For those unaccustomed to Japan, *horigotatsu* and the substitution cooked dishes for raw fish in the course menus (must be requested in advance) will make things more comfortable. It is better to make reservations.

World Town Bldg. 5-8-17 Ginza, Chuo-ku ☎ 3574-8806 S Ginza Sta. ◷ 11:30-22:00 H None ¥★★★ C JCB, DN, VISA, MC, AMEX, others

ASAKUSA-IMAHAN

ZAKURO	17
ざくろ	G4

Although actually a traditional Japanese restaurant, Zakuro is famed for its *shabu shabu*. The special flavor comes from the authentic charcoal fire over which the deluxe marbled Kobe roast is cooked. The *kimono*-clad waitresses give excellent service. *Shabu shabu* set menus begin at ¥9,800. Reservations are necessary for private rooms.

Nihon Jitensha Kaikan, 1-9-15 Akasaka, Minato-ku ☎ 3582-2661 S Toranomon Sta. ◷ 11:00-15:00, 17:30-23:00 H None ¥★★★ C JCB, DN, VISA, MC, AMEX, others

ZENPEI

MANSEI 29 万世 H4

This beef restaurant is located in front of the Transportation Museum in Kanda, right by Manseibashi Bridge. The restaurant is undergoing renovation (open in '91 summer) so business continues as usual at this temporary shop. *Sukiyaki* and *shabu shabu* (from ¥4,100) are just a part of a diverse menu including steak (from ¥1,750) and hamburgers from choice Japanese beef. The portions are large and everything is delicious.
2-21 Kanda-Sudacho, Chiyoda-ku ☎ 3251-0291 ⑤ JR Akihabara Sta. ⊙ 11:00-21:00 ℍ None ¥★★ ℂ JCB, DN, VISA, MC, others

YONEKYU 32 米久 C2

This *gyu-nabe* (a type of *sukiyaki*) restaurant opened in Asakusa's commercial district in 1885. It was popular among the literary crowd including turn-of-the-century poet Kotaro Takamura. Prices are as low as you would expect in Asakusa. *Nabe* with egg and vegetables is ¥2,400 to ¥3, 600 per person (rice is available for an additional charge).
2-17-10 Asakusa, Taito-ku ☎ 3841-6416 ⑤ Asakusa Sta. ⊙ 12:00-21:00 ℍ 1st Tue. ¥★★ ℂ JCB, DN, VISA, MC, AMEX, others

ZENPEI 12 禅平 B2

This *teppanyaki* restaurant specializes in beef, served in a tasteful modern decor. Complete courses of hors d'œuvres, seafood, Kobe beef *teppanyaki*, rice, and dessert run from ¥8,000 to ¥13,000. The cooks, working directly in front of you, put on a remarkable display of skill.
Fukuda Bldg. 8-6-8 Ginza, Chuo-ku ☎ 3574-0310 ⑤ JR Shinbashi Sta. ⊙ 11:30-14;00, 17:00-2:00 ℍ None ¥★★★ ℂ JCB, DN, VISA, MC, AMEX, others

EATING & DRINKING

ECHIKATSU	江知勝	2-31-23 Yushima, Bunkyo-ku	☎3811-5293	31・A6
OKAHAN	岡半	7-6-16 Ginza, Chuo-Ku	☎3571-1417	12・B2
IMAASA	今朝	1-1-21 Higashi-shinbashi, Minato-ku	☎3572-5286	12・A3
MAYA	摩耶	Hibiya Bldg. 1-1-1 Shinbashi, Minato-ku	☎3591-0633	12・A1
MATSUKIYA	松喜屋	2-26-10 Shiroganedai, Minato-ku	☎3449-0298	14・C4
HASEJIN	はせ甚	3-3-15 Azabudai, Minato-ku	☎3582-7811	16・D6
ISSHIN	一心	Sugimoto Bldg. 4-21-29 Minami-aoyama, Minato-ku	☎3401-4611	23・G5
YOSHIHASHI	よしはし	1-5-25 Motoakasaka Minato-ku	☎3401-3129	17・E1

GINZA TEN-ICHI(Main Shop) | 12
銀座天一 | C3

This elegant *tempura* restaurant has even served guests of state. Its role in converting *tempura* from a cheap plebeian dish to the refined meal it has become cannot be ignored. The delicious food they have been serving in Ginza for half a century is without equal. Part of the attraction is to sit at the counter and eat the hot *tempura* fried right before your eyes. The set menus start at ¥7,000 for lunch and ¥12,000 or ¥15,000 for dinner. Reservations are necessary in the evening.

6-6-5 Ginza (Namiki-dori), Chuo-ku ☎ 3571-1272 S Ginza Sta. ◎ 11:30-21:30 H None ¥ ★ ★ ★ ★ C JCB, DN, VISA, MC, AMEX, others

HANAMURA | 17
花むら | E3

The freshest ingredients of each season are fried in a special iron pot right at your seat. The *tentsuyu* (sauce for dipping *tempura*) contains only the best dried bonito flakes and kelp broth. Set menus start at ¥5,500.

6-6-5 Akasaka, Minato-ku ☎ 3585-4570 S Akasaka Sta. ◎ 12:00-22:00 H Tue. ¥ ★ ★ ★ C JCB, DN, VISA, MC, AMEX

GINZA TENKUNI | 12
銀座天國 | B3

To celebrate the 100th anniversary of its founding, Tenkuni moved into a modern building but the traditional flavor has not altered with time. The *tempura* is fried in fragrant sesame oil, giving it a sharper taste and darker color than is usual. In addition to *tempura* courses which begin at ¥8,000, *tendon* [*tempura* on rice] starts at ¥1,400 and *tempura teishoku* [rice, miso soup and pickled vegetables] at ¥2,500. At lunch you can get *tendon* for ¥900.

8-9-11 Ginza, Chuo-ku ☎ 3571-1092 S JR Shinbashi Sta. ◎ 11:30-22:00 H 1st & 3rd Wed. ¥ ★ ★ ★ C JCB, DN, VISA, MC, AMEX, others

TSUNAHACHI | 27
つな八 | E3

As the largest *tempura* chain in Japan, Tsunahachi has been able to secure their own sources for ingredients. Through the efforts of the management, they are able to offer delicious traditional *tempura* at low prices. A set meal with all different kinds of *tempura* can be had for under ¥2,000.

3-31-8 Shinjuku, Shinjuku-ku ☎ 3352-1012 S JR Shinjuku Sta. ◎ 11:30-22:30 H None ¥ ★ C JCB, VISA, AMEX

TENMASA	天政	2-6-8 Sarugaku-Cho, Chiyoda-ku	☎3291-4480	28·C3
HAYASHI	はやし	1-12-10 Nihonbashi Muromachi,Chuo-ku	☎3241-5367	19·F5
HASHIZEN	橋善	1-7-11 Shinbashi, Minato-ku	☎3571-2700	12·A3
UOSHIN	魚新	Hanazawa Bldg, 5-5-8 Roppongi, Minato-ku	☎3403-1051	16·C6
TSURUOKA	つる岡	4-31-3 Jingumae Shibuya-ku	☎3408-4061	22·C5
DAIKOKUYA	大黒屋	1-38-10 Asakusa Taito-ku	☎3844-1111	32·B3
MASARU	まさる	1-32-2 Asakusa Taito-ku	☎3841-8356	32·B3
YAMASHITA	山下	2-14-30 Ueno, Taito-ku	☎3831-7810	31·C5

KANDA-YABU

KANDA-YABU	29
神田藪	G4

Yabu is one of the several schools of traditional *soba* making in Tokyo and Kanda-Yabu might be called its headquarters. Eating the firm *soba* in the slightly salt broth inside the bamboo grove surrounded by a board fence brings one back to the days when Tokyo was called Edo. Plain *soba*, drained (*seiro*) or in soup (*kake*) is ¥550 while *tempura soba* is ¥1,300.

2-10 Kanda-Awajicho, Chiyoda-ku ☎ 3251-0287 [S] Shin-Ochanomizu Sta., Ogawamachi Sta., Awajicho Sta. ⊙ 11:30-19:00 [H] Mon [¥] ★ [C] None

KANDA-YABU

MUROMACHI-SUNABA	19
室町砂場	H3

This *soba* shop is just about as prominent as Kanda-yabu. It is distinguished by the salty soup, stubbornly protecting the traditional Tokyo *soba* flavor. Although now universally popular, this shop devised *tenzaru soba* (drained *soba* with *tempura*) more than forty years ago.

4-1-13 Nihonbashi-Muromachi, Chuo-ku ☎ 3241-4038 [JR] Shin-Nihonbashi Sta. [S] Mitsukoshimae Sta. ⊙ 11:00-19:30 (Sat.-19:00) [H] Sun., hol. [¥] ★ [C] None

MIMIU	13
美々卯	E4

Udon is to Kansai what *soba* is to Kanto and thus the Mimiu main shop is in Osaka. Mimiu's original specialty is *Udonsuki*, shrimp, chicken and vegetables boiled in a mild soup with *udon*. It is as popular in Tokyo as it is in Osaka. Courses such as *udonsuki* and *sashimi* run from ¥3,000 to ¥9,000.

3-6-4 Kyobashi, Chuo-ku ☎ 3567-6571 [S] Takaracho Sta., Kyobashi Sta. ⊙ 11:30-20:30 (Sun. & hol. -20:00) [H] 1st & 3rd Sun. [¥] ★★ [C] None

●SOBA

SOHONKE-SARASHINA-HORII	総本家更科堀井	3-11-4 Motoazabu, Minato-ku	☎3403-3401	16・B6
IKENOHATA- YABUSOBA	池の端藪蕎麦	3-44-7 Yushima, Bunkyo-ku	☎3831-8977	31・C5
MATSUYA	まつや	1-13 Kanda Suda-cho, Chiyoda-ku	☎3251-1556	29・G4
YOSHIDA	よし田	7-7-8 Ginza, Chuo-ku	☎3571-0526	12・B3
OWARIYA	尾張屋	1-7-1 Asakusa, Taito-ku	☎3845-4500	32・B2
IZUMOSOBA-HONKE	出雲そば本家	1-51 Kanda Jinbo-cho, Chiyoda-ku	☎3291-3005	28・D5

●UDON

CHOTOKU	長徳	1-10-5 Shibuya, Shibuya-ku	☎3407-8891	25・G2
SANGOKUICHI	三国一	3-24-8 Shinjuku, Shinjuku-ku	☎3354-3591	27・E2

Other Japanese Foods

TSUJITOME	17
辻留	E1

Kaiseki cuisine developed from the tea ceremony. This is one of the most prominent restaurants serving this elegant full-course meal. Mr. Tsuji, the owner, is also renowned as the author of many cookbooks. Only the best ingredients are brought directly from all over the country and prepared with a light hand to preserve their delicate flavors. Lunch courses start at ¥20,000 and dinner at ¥27,000. Although expensive, it is well worth the cost. Reservations are necessary.

Toraya 2nd Bldg., 1-5-8 Moto-Akasaka, Minato-ku ☎ 3403-3984 S Akasaka-mitsuke Sta. ◷ 12:00-21:00 H Sun (there are exceptions too) ¥ ★★★ C JCB, DN, VISA, MC, AMEX, others

TENTAKE	12
天竹	B6

Blowfish is a delicacy only eaten in winter but at Tentake it is served around the year at affordable prices. Dishes like raw blowfish (¥3,200) and blowfish stew (from ¥3,200) are complemented by *hirezake*, sake seasoned with grilled blowfish fin. Courses start at ¥7,700. About 200 people can be seated but even this immense capacity does not keep up with its popularity and there are always lines. Eel is added to the menu during the summer.

6-16-6 Tsukiji, Chuo-ku ☎ 3541-3881 S Tsukiji Sta. ◷ 12:00-22:00 H Apr.-Sept.: Sun; Oct., Nov., Feb., Mar: 1st & 3rd Wed.; Dec., Jan.: Dec. 31 and Jan. 1 only. ¥ ★★★ C None

KUSHIHACHI	16
串八	C5

The traditional interior of the restaurant contains a courtyard and *yakitori* (grilled chicken on skewers) can be enjoyed around the hearth. A set of four side dishes and twelve skewers starts at ¥7,000.

Kajikawa-seishido Bldg. 3-10-9 Roppongi, Minato-ku ☎ 3403-3060 S Roppongi Sta. ◷ 17:30-23:00 H Sun. ¥ ★★★ C JCB, DN, VISA, MC, AMEX, others

NANBANTEI	16
南蛮亭	C5

In addition to Roppongi, branches of this affordable *yakitori* restaurant can be found all over Tokyo. *Asuparamaki* (asparagus wrapped in beef) and *shisomaki* (chicken wrapped in perilla leaves) (¥480 for 2 skewers), are also available. A ¥3,000 course (13 skewers of 9 different kinds) and a ¥3,500 course (14 items of 10 different kinds) are available.

4-5-6 Roppongi, Minato-ku ☎ 3402-0606 S Roppongi Sta. ◷ 17:00-23:30 H None ¥ ★★ C JCB, DN, VISA, MC, AMEX, others

CHIKUYOTEI (Main Shop)	12
竹葉亭	B4

Eel is a favorite food in Japan, especially during the summer. The famed Chikuyotei offers *kabayaki* (grilled eel with sweetened soy sauce), and *shiroyaki* (plain-grilled) as well as the more affordable *unaju* (*kabayaki* on rice, from ¥2,000). Private rooms are also available (reservations necessary).

8-14-7 Ginza, Chuo-ku ☎ 3542-0787 S Higashi-Ginza Sta. ◷ 11:30-14:00, 16:30-20:00 H Sun. and hol. ¥ ★★ C None

KOMAGATA DOJYOU

	32
駒形どぜう	A3

Few restaurants serve loach but this one is very popular. The ingredients, cooking methods and interior have remained the same for decades. In addition to *miso*-flavor loach stew (¥1,100) and the eggy *yanagawa nabe* (¥1,100), the *kabayaki* loach, prepared like eel, is also delicious.

1-7-12 Komagata, Taito-ku ☎ 3842-4001 [S] Asakusa Sta. ⊙ 11:00-21:00 [H] None [¥] ★★ [C] JCB, DN, VISA, others

OTAKO (Main Shop)

	12
お多幸	C3

Located in an alley behind the Ginza Sony Building. *Oden* is representative of plebeian eating habits. It consists of *nerimono* (items made of fish paste), *daikon*, *tofu*, eggs and lots of other things steeped in a highly seasoned soy-based sauce. Prices start at ¥150 each and a plate of four is ¥750.

5-4-16 Ginza, Chuo-ku ☎ 3571-0057 [S] Ginza Sta. ⊙ 16:30-22:30 [H] Sun. & hol. [¥] ★ [C] None

YOTARO

	17
与太呂	F2

Yotaro is unusual in that they specialize in sea bream. *Taimeshi* is their most popular dish. Sea bream brought from the Inland Sea is steamed in an earthenware pot with rice. The diner is shown the completed dish before the sea bream is cut into pieces, mixed with the rice and served. A course with *taimeshi*, *sashimi* and *tempura* is available for ¥12,000 per person. Reservations are necessary.

Akasakakan-Arai Bldg. 3-12-18 Akasaka, Minato-ku ☎ 3584-7686 [S] Akasaka Sta. ⊙ 12:00-13:30, 17:30-22:30 [H] Sun [¥] ★★★★ [C] JCB, DN, VISA, MC, AMEX, others

KOMAGATA DOJYOU

SHIMAZUTEI

	12
島津亭	C2

The cuisine of the Kagoshima area in southern Japan is served in a traditional setting. Herring-like *kibinago*, *satsu 'a age* (fried fish paste and vegetables), chicken and other ingredients are flown in fresh each day. A course offering a full sampling is ¥7,000.

Iijima Bldg.2nd 6-4-8 Ginza, Chuo-ku ☎ 3574-6088 [S] Ginza Sta. ⊙ 17:00-22:00 [H] Sun. and hol. [¥] ★★★ [C] JCB, DN, VISA, MC, AMEX, others

ISARIBI

	12
いさりび	B2

Hokkaido is known for having delicious food. This restaurant offers local Hokkaido delicacies at very reasonable prices. Unusual croquettes made with salmon and *Sanpeijiru* (soup with salmon and vegetables) are just a few of the treats that await you. Most items are ¥500.

8-6-2 Ginza, Chuo-ku ☎ 3571-3923 [S] [JR] Shinbashi Sta. ⊙ 17:00-2:00 (Sat. -22:00) [H] Sun. and hol. [¥] ★★ [C] JCB, DN, VISA, MC, AMEX, others

EATING & DRINKING

GINZA-ISOMURA | 12
銀座磯むら | C4

This counter-only restaurant serves *kushiage* — meat, fish, or vegetables threaded on a skewer and deep-fried. Thirty different kinds of fresh ingredients are always available. The cook paces himself by how fast you eat so your *kushiage* are always at their piping hot best. Courses with 14 skewers, *sashimi*, and salad start at ¥5,300. This is also a popular place for lunch.

Central Bldg. 4-10-3 Ginza, Chuo-ku ☎ 3546-6964 [S] Ginza Sta. ◷ 10:30-21:30 [H] None ¥★★ [C] JCB, DN, VISA, MC, AMEX, others

TONKATSU IMOYA | 28
いもや | D4

A slice of pork roast with just the right amount of fat is fried crispy and served with lots of cabbage, *miso* soup and rice is just ¥600. The sister shop, Tempura-Imoya is right near by and is just as cheap and delicious. Both are extremely popular with local students.

2-48 Kanda Jinbo-cho, Chiyoda-ku ☎ 3265-0922 [S] Jinbocho Sta. ◷ 11:00-20:00 [H] Sun (except for 3rd Sun.) ¥★ [C] None

TARUYA | 24
たるや | C5

Shibuya is a favorite spot among the youth of Tokyo and this *okonomiyaki* restaurant is right in the heart of it. *Okonomiyaki* is made differently in different regions and Taruya has them all. *Okonomiyaki* runs ¥550-600 each. Fried meat or vegetables is ¥400-900. Prices are low and the atmosphere relaxing.

2-20-6 Dogenzaka, Shibuya-ku ☎ 3461-3325 [S] [JR] Shibuya Sta. ◷ 17:00-23:30 [H] Sun. ¥★ [C] None

TONKI | 14
とんき | B4

Tonkatsu, or slices of pork coated and then deep-fried in oil, is a Japanese adaptation of western cuisine. This restaurant is stands out even among the many *tonkatsu* restaurants in Tokyo. Of course the delicious black pig is the main reason but the beautiful white wood counter and excellent service also contribute to Tonki's popularity. Roast and fillet *tonkatsu teishoku* with rice, *miso* soup and pickled vegetables can be had for ¥1,450 each.

1-1-2 Shimo-Meguro, Meguro-ku ☎ 3491-9928 [JR] Meguro Sta. ◷ 16:00-22:45 [H] Tue. and 3rd Mon. ¥★ [C] DN, VISA

GINZA-ISOMURA

HANABISHI | 12
葉名菱 | C4

Okonomiyaki, flour and water mixed with a variety of fillings and fried, is a favorite plebian snack. This restaurant is located behind the Kabuki-za Theater and is always crowded with young people from neighboring offices. A perfect place for a relaxing evening with friends.

4-12-3 Ginza, Chuo-ku ☎ 3541-2877 [S] Ginza Sta. ◷ 17:00-22:00 (Sat. 13:00-22:00 Sun. & hol. 13:00-20:00) [H] None ¥★ [C] None

HOKABEN–WHEN YOU'RE LOOKING FOR A CHEAP LUNCH

Walking through Tokyo, one frequently comes across *bento* (boxed lunch) stands. They are popularly called *Hokaben*. At lunch time, office workers frequently line up in front of them. Almost all are chains with names like Hokahoka Bento and Takitate. Salmon, laver and rice, chicken, curry — the menus are diverse but the main attraction is the prices. Salmon or laver lunches can be had for less than ¥400. Young workers buy these lunches and eat them in the office to make their paychecks last a little longer.

●JAPANESE DISHES

TOYODA	とよ田	1-12 Nihonbashi Muromachi, Chuo-ku	☎3241-1025	**19·F5**
WABISUKE	侘助	Nogizaka Place, 9-6-30 Akasaka, Minato-ku	☎3408-8825	**16·C3**

●LOCAL SPECIALTIES

SAIKAI	西海	2-8-5 Uchikanda, Chiyoda-ku	☎3254-6557	**29·G6**
NAGASAKIRO	長崎楼	Harada Bldg. 1-14 Nihonbashi Muromachi, Chuo-ku	☎3241-0061	**19·F5**
NEBOKE	祢保希	3-11-17 Akasaka, Minato-ku	☎3585-9640	**17·F2**

●CHICKEN DISHES

ISEKO	伊勢広	1-5-4 Kyobashi, Chuo-ku	☎3281-5864	**18·A3**
TORITOMO	酉友	Jubankan Bldg. 10 Araki-cho, Shinjuku-ku	☎3357-6789	**27·H5**
TAMAHIDE	玉ひで	1-17-10 Nihonbashi Ningyo-cho, Chuo-ku	☎3668-7651	**19·F6**

●GRILLED EEL

KANDAGAWA	神田川	2-5-11 Sotokanda, Chiyoda-ku	☎3251-5031	**29·G2**
KANDA-KIKUKAWA	神田きくかわ	1-24-2 Kanda Suda-cho, Chiyoda-ku	☎3254-3895	**29·H5**
MIYAKAWA-HONTEN	宮川本廛	1-4-6 Tsukiji, Chuo-ku	☎3541-1292	**12·D6**

●TONKATSU

FUTABA	双葉	2-8-11 Ueno, Taito-ku	☎3831-6483	**31·C5**
TONKATSU-MAISEN	とんかつ まい泉	4-8-5 Jingumae Shibuya-ku	☎3470-0071	**23·E4**
KATORI	香とり	1-6-4 Hanakawado Taito-ku	☎3844-2290	**32·B3**

●OKONOMIYAKI

UTAJAYA	歌茶屋	2-11-13 Ginza, Chuo-ku	☎3541-7583	**12·D4**

●NATURAL FOODS

MOMINOKI HOUSE	モミノキハウス	You Bldg. 2-18-5 Jingumae, Shibuya-ku	☎3405-9144	**22·C3**

EATING & DRINKING

KIRAKU	24
喜楽	D5

This authentic *ramen* noodle restaurant first opened its doors in 1953. The soy sauce-flavor soup is made from pork and chicken bones. *Chukamen* (¥520) [*ramen* with an egg boiled in the juices of roast pork] is one of their most popular items. Other popular dishes are *moyashimen* (¥620) [noodles with beans sprouts] and *gyoza* (¥450) [pork dumplings].

2-17-6 Dogenzaka, Shibuya-ku ☎ 3461-2032 Ⓢ ⒿⓇ Shibuya Sta. ⊙ 11:30-20:00 Ⓗ Wed. ¥ ★ Ⓒ None

KAPPAKEN	–
河童軒	–

Located in the student quarter near Waseda Univ. The building also contains a movie theater. At lunch time a line forms to eat here. *Kappamen* (¥650) with an egg on top, and the spicy *karakaramen* (¥650) might be part of the reason for this popularity.

Inamon Bldg. 2-18-11 Takadanobaba, Shinjuku-ku ☎ 3200-5069 Ⓢ ⒿⓇ Takadanobaba Sta. ⊙ 11:00-23:00 Ⓗ None ¥ ★ Ⓒ None

KEIKA	27
桂花	F3

Keika offers the *ramen* of Kyushu where the noodles are eaten hard and the broth is milky white from pork bones. Although very different from the usual *ramen* shop, *Hakata ramen* can be addictive. The menu includes *Keika ramen* (¥520) and Ta low men (¥780) which contains pork and cabbage.

3-7-2 Shinjuku, Shinjuku-ku ☎ 3354-4591 Ⓢ ⒿⓇ Shinjuku Sta. ⊙ 11:00-22:45 Ⓗ None ¥ ★ Ⓒ None

DAIHACHI	16
大八	C4

Located right across the street from the Ministry of Defense. The chicken stock is rich but no oil has been added to keep it light. There are only ten counter seats which are always full at night with young people on their way home from a night of fun in Roppongi. *Ramen* is ¥500 and won ton men is ¥700.

7-12-1 Roppongi, Minato-ku ☎ 3405-0721 Ⓢ Roppongi Sta. ⊙ 18:00-2:00 Ⓗ Sun.& hol. ¥ ★ Ⓒ None

CHAIN RAMEN SHOPS

Chinese noodles, or *ramen*, can be eaten quickly and cheaply. Its ubiquity makes it one of Japan's most popular fast foods so it is no surprise chain restaurants should develop. Competition keeps prices down and the food good so you can safely enjoy a meal at a *ramen* chain no matter where you are. Some of the largest chains include Dosanko (*miso ramen*, salt *ramen*, ¥450 each), and Sapporoya (soy sauce *ramen*, salt *ramen*, ¥490 each) for Hokkaido-style *ramen* and Fukuchan (*ramen* ¥500) for Kyushu-style *ramen*.

TOKOEN	12
東興園	C2

Set deep in an alley in a corner of Ginza. The meaty *shumai* dumplings (¥600), fried rice (¥850) and *ramen* (¥650) are popular. Ingredients are carefully selected for delicious results.

7-3-16 Ginza, Chuo-ku ☎ 3571-5065 S Ginza Sta. ⊙ 11:30-20:30 H Sun. & hol.¥★ C None

GINZA ASTER (South Ginza Branch)	12
銀座アスター	C3

This renowned Chinese restaurant chain has branches all over town. Their menu is enormous, ranging from simple noodle dishes to the most complex delicacies. Private rooms are available for gatherings. The Ginza Main Shop is being renovated. *Ramen* is ¥1,200 while *shumai* are ¥1,000.

Midori Bldg. 5-9-11 Ginza, Chuo-ku ☎ 3571-4550 S Ginza Sta. ⊙ 11:30-22:00 H None¥★★★ C JCB, DN, VISA, MC, AMEX, others

SHISEN HANTEN	17
四川飯店	G1

There are many regional styles of cooking in China. Szechwan (Shisen) is known for being heavily seasoned and spicy but this is not necessarily the case at Shisenhanten. There are chicken, beef, shrimp and other dishes to suit a variety of palates. Banbanji (a chicken dish) is ¥1,800 and Kopa (rice gruel) is ¥2,800.

Zenkoku Ryokan Kaikan, 2-5-5 Hirakawa-cho, Chiyoda-ku ☎ 3263-9371 S Nagatacho Sta. ⊙ 11:30-14:30, 17:00-22:00 (Sun. & hol. 11:30-22:00) H None ¥★★★ C JCB, DN, VISA, MC, AMEX, others

SHODOTEN	18
小洞天	D4

Delicious meat dumplings called *shumai* are a popular dish in Japan and the specialty of this shop. They are larger than the usual and mildly sweet. Take-out is available. At lunch try the *shumai* lunch set (¥720).

1-2-17 Nihonbashi, Chuo-ku ☎ 3272-1071 S Nihonbashi Sta. ⊙ 11:00-15:00, 17:00-21:00 (Sat. 11:00-20:00) H Sun. & hol. ¥★ C JCB, DN, VISA, MC, AMEX, others

SETSUEN

SETSUEN	27
雪園	G3

One of the few Hunan restaurants in Tokyo. Although similar to Szechwan cooking, Hunan cuisine is seasoned a little less heavily which makes it easier to eat. In addition to the chicken and duck dishes you might expect, frogs are also included on the menu. Kausufan (something like a sandwich) is ¥1,600. Try the frogs at ¥3,000. It is better to make reservations.

3-8-9 Shinjuku, Shinjuku-ku ☎ 3354-4028 S JR Shinjuku Sta. ⊙ 11:30-14:00, 17:30-22:00 H Sun. ¥★★★ C JCB, DN, VISA, MC, AMEX, others

HEICHINRO | 24

聘珍樓 | D2

The main shop in Yokohama China Town has been in business for more than a hundred years and this proud tradition is faithfully continued in Tokyo. The abundant menu contains sharks fin and many other soups and lots of stir-fried meat and vegetables. The stylish interior encourages leisurely dining. Lunches start at ¥700 and courses are from ¥4,000.

Shibuya Hillside Bldg. 1-19-3 Jinnan, Shibuya-ku ☎ 3464-7888 S JR Shibuya Sta. ⏰ 11:00-22:30 H None ¥★★★ C JCB, DN, VISA, MC, AMEX, others

KENKO CHUSHINTEKI-YAMUCHA HONPO

KENKO CHUSHINTEKI-YAMUCHA HONPO | 25

健康中心的飲茶本舗 | H2

The name is long but the restaurant is comfortable. *Yamucha* is a type of Chinese cooking based mostly on snacks like steamed and fried dumplings. At this Canton-type Yamucha restaurant each item is ¥200-300 so you can eat lots of different dishes.

2-8-10 Shibuya, Shibuya-ku ☎ 3498-8132 S JR Shibuya Sta. ⏰ 17:00-22:00 H Sun., hol., 1st, 3rd and 5th Sat. ¥★ C None

LITTLE HONG KONG | 31

リトル香港 | B6

Shanghai cuisine prepared with fresh seafood, meat and vegetables. Many of the ingredients are imported from China to keep the taste as authentic as possible. The boiled shark's fin (¥4,000 each) is delicious. Lunch is quite inexpensive, with set lunches from ¥850 and noodles from ¥750.

3-38-9 Yushima, Bunkyo-ku ☎ 3831-2638 S Yushima Sta., Ueno-hirokoji Sta. ⏰ 11:30-23:00 (Sun. & hol. -22:30) H None ¥★★★ C JCB, DN, VISA, MC, AMEX, others

AKASAKA-MINMIN | 16

赤坂珉々 | C2

A diverse menu offering everything from fried dumplings and noodles to full courses. The *ramen* (¥400), with extra thin noodles and soup made from whole chicken, is especially popular.

8-7-14 Akasaka, Minato-ku ☎ 3408-4805 S Nogizaka Sta. ⏰ 12:00-14:00, 17:00-22:00 H Sun ¥★★ C JCB, DN, VISA, MC, AMEX, others

TOKARIN | 17

桃花林 | G5

Canton Chinese cuisine contains some of the most exquisite culinary delights found in Chinese cooking and this restaurant can provide a great deal of this abundant regional flavor. Rare delicacies like bear paws, whole roast piglet, and turtle soup fill the menu. Located in the Main Wing of the Hotel Okura. Lunch is ¥2,300 and dinner is ¥9,000.

2-10-4 Toranomon, Minato-ku ☎ 3505-6068 S Kamiyacho Sta., Toranomon Sta. ⏰ 11:30-14:30, 17:30-22:00 (Tea time is from 13:00-16:00 on weekdays and 11:30-16:00 on weekends and hol.) H None ¥★★★ C JCB, DN, VISA, MC, AMEX, others

REIKYO | 24 | D4
麗郷

Taiwanese cooking is popular in Japan but this restaurant has an exceptional number of fans. One of the first Taiwanese restaurants in Tokyo, it has been operating in Shibuya since right after the end of World War II. As you enter, you are immediately struck by the stuffed intestines hanging from the ceiling. They are delicious, complementing beer and Chinese liquor. Try the stir-fried garlic stalks (¥1,000) and the *ramen* noodles (¥900).

2-25-18 Dogenzaka, Shibuya-ku ☎ 3464-8617 S JR Shibuya Sta. ⏰ 12:00-14:00, 17:00-1:00 (Sat., Sun., and hol., 12:00-01:00 a.m.) H Thur. ¥ ★★ C None

REIKYO

BAIEN | 27 | F1
梅園

This Taiwanese restaurant is located in a corner of Tokyo's largest amusement quarter, Shinjuku-Kabukicho. The Taiwanese cook makes everything to suit Japanese tastes. Taiwanese stuffed intestines (¥700) and corbicula with soy sauce are favorites.

2-26-3 Kabukicho, Shinjuku-ku ☎ 3200-3136 S JR Shinjuku Sta. ⏰ 17:00-04:00 (Sun. & hol. -23:00) H None ¥★★ C JCB, DN, VISA, MC, AMEX, others

GOJUBAN | — | —
五十番

People come from all over for these big hand-made steamed buns. Stuffed with delicious meat and vegetables, they really fill you up. Meat buns (¥250), *Gomoku* (meat and vegetable) (¥500) and roast pork (¥500) are some of the most popular of the 15 different kinds. You can eat them there or take them out.

3-2 Kagurazaka, Shinjuku-ku ☎ 3260-0066 S JR Kagurazaka Sta. ⏰ 10:00-23:00 H Tue. ¥★ C None

●RAMEN

HOPU-KEN	ホープ軒	2-33-9 Sendagaya, Shibuya-ku ☎3405-4249	22・C1
KAZUKI	香月	Honma.Bldg,1-10-8 Ebisu-nishi,☎3496-6885 Shibuya-ku	14・A2
NAKAMOTO	中本	Yurakucho bldg. 1-10-1 ☎3213-8489 Yurakucho, Chiyoda-ku	12・D2
MANPUKU	萬福	2-13-13 Ginza, Chuo-ku ☎3541-7210	12・D5

●CHINESE DISHES

CHUGOKU-HANTEN	中國飯店	5-13-18 Shiba, Minato-ku ☎3798-1381	15・E2
SUIEN-SARO	翠園茶楼	Hibiya Kokusai Bldg. 2-2-3 ☎3595-0091 Uchisaiwai-cho, Chiyoda-ku	12・B1
TSUKIJI-SHINKYOTEI	築地新橋亭	1-12-6 Tsukiji, Chuo-ku ☎3543-1041	12・C5
TOKYO-DAIHANTEN	東京大飯店	5-17-13 Shinjuku, Shinjuku-ku ☎3202-0121	27・F2

MAXIM'S DE PARIS | 12

| マキシム・ド・パリ | D3 |

Located in the basement of the Ginza Sony Bldg. The interior and menu of the Paris original have been reproduced en bloc. Light lunch courses start at ¥6,600 and full course dinners from ¥20,000. The excellent wine selection is complimented by cheeses and spices are imported directly from France. Reservations are necessary for dinner.

Sony Bldg. 5-3-1 Ginza, Chuo-ku ☎ 3572-3621 Ⓢ Ginza Sta. ◷ 11:30-14:30, 17:30-22:00 Ⓗ Sun. Ⓨ★★★★ Ⓒ DN, VISA, MC, AMEX

BRASSERIE BERNARD | 16

| ブラスリー・ベルナール | C5 |

A brasserie is a cafe-style place for drinking beer and wine and eating the foods that go with them. It's more casual than a restaurant, but the food — in Bernard's case at least — matches that of any popularly priced Parisian restaurant. Lunch courses from ¥1,200; dinner is a la carte and features mostly Provençal specialties.

7-14-3 Roppongi, Minato-ku ☎ 3405-7877 Ⓢ Roppongi Sta. ◷ 11:30-14:00, 17:30-24:30 Ⓗ None Ⓨ★★ Ⓒ JCB, DN, VISA, MC, AMEX, others

LA TOUR D'ARGENT | 17

| ラ・トゥール・ダルジャン | F1 |

The only branch of the famed Michelin three star restaurant on the banks of the Seine in Paris. The authentic preparations by the French chef and interior modeled after the original make you feel as if you were dining in Paris. The menu changes with the season. Set menus start at ¥17,000. Reservations are necessary.

Hotel New Otani, Main Building Lobby 2F 4-1 Kioi-cho, Chiyoda-ku ☎ 3239-3111 Ⓢ Akasaka-mitsuke Sta. ◷ 17:30-22:00 Ⓗ None Ⓨ★★★★ Ⓒ DN, VISA, MC, AMEX

BAIN MARIE | 29

| ばん・まりー | H4 |

A lively restaurant that would not be out of place in Paris. In addition to the a la carte menu, four full courses ranging in price from ¥3,500 to ¥8,500 are also offered. Each provides an authentic taste of Paris from the hors d'œuvre, to the meat and fish and through the dessert. It is better to make reservations.

1 Kanda-Iwamotocho, Chiyoda-ku ☎ 3251-6106 ⒿⓇ Akihabara Sta. Ⓢ Iwamotocho Sta. ◷ 11:00-15:00, 17:00-21:00 Ⓗ Sun. & hol. Ⓨ★★ Ⓒ JCB, DN, VISA, UC

BRASSERIE BERNARD

CLAIR D' AKASAKA | 17
クレール・ド・赤坂 | F3

Perched on the 19th floor of the Nissho Iwai Bldg., you can enjoy a view of the National Diet and Imperial Palace from the main dining room. Our recommendation is the ¥22,000 course menu with abalone steak as the main course. Three business lunch courses are offered at ¥3,500. Other popular options include Omi beef and seafood from the sea off Japan. Reservations are necessary for private rooms and window seats.

2-4-5 Akasaka, Minato-ku ☎ 3583-3570 [S] Akasaka-mitsuke Sta. [⏱] 11:30-14:00, 17:30-22:00 (Sat. -21:00) [H] Sun. & hol. [¥] ★★★★ [C] DN, VISA, MC, AMEX

ILE DE FRANCE

ILE DE FRANCE | 16
イル・ド・フランス | C5

The Carcassone-born owner opened this restaurant in Japan more than twenty years ago and has been serving provencal cuisine ever since. Lunch courses are ¥2,700 while dinner courses range from ¥6,000 to ¥10,000. Each course allows you to select an entree and main dish from several offerings.

3-11-5 Roppongi, Minato-ku ☎ 3404-0384 [S] Roppongi Sta. [⏱] 11:30-14:00, 17:30-22:00 [H] Sun. [¥] ★★★ [C] DN, VISA, MC, AMEX

QUEEN ALICE | 20
クィーン・アリス | D1

A new type of French restaurant looking to create post-Nouvelle Cuisine. No a la carte. Lunches start at ¥3,500 and dinners at ¥7,500. One of the few detached houses in the Minato ward area, the abundance of verdure, both inside and out, provide a tranquil setting to enjoy your meal.

3-17-34 Nishi-Azabu, Minato-ku ☎ 3405-9039 [S] Roppongi Sta. [⏱] 12:00-15:00, 18:00-22:30 [H] None [¥] ★★★ [C] DN, VISA, AMEX

AU MILIEU	オ・ミリュー	6-1-26 Roppongi, Minato-ku	☎3401-8476	**16・C5**
ISOLDE	イゾルデ	3-2-1 Nishi-azabu, Minato-ku	☎3478-1055	**16・B5**
LE COUPE CHOU	ル・クープ・シュー	1-15-7 Nishi-shinjuku, Shinjuku-ku	☎3348-1610	**26・C3**
BISTRO LA POSTE	ビストロ・ラ・ポスト	2-5-7 Hirakawa-cho, Chiyoda-ku	☎3262-0743	**27・G1**
KYOTO YUTAKA	京都 ゆたか	2-3 Yaesu, Chuo-ku	☎3281-0546	**18・A3**
CHEZ INNO	シェ・イノ	3-2-11 Kyobashi, Chuo-ku	☎3274-2020	**13・E4**
LE TOUCAN	ル・トゥカン	8-6-3 Ginza, Chuo-ku	☎3575-4142	**12・B2**
MIKAWAYA	みかわや	4-7-16 Ginza, Chuo-ku	☎3561-2006	**12・C4**

CARMINE

カルミネ

–
–

Carmine is the chef and owner of this restaurant. He was born in southern Italy and studied cooking in Florence, arriving in Japan in 1977. The menu contains representative items from all over Italy. Courses start at ¥1,500 for lunch and ¥3,500 for dinner. These prices are quite low considering the food is authentic and the servings generous. Reservations are necessary.

21 Nakamachi, Shinjuku-ku ☎ 3260-5066 S Kagurazaka Sta. ⏰ 12:00-14:00, 18:00-23:00 H Sun. ¥★ C None

ARAGOSTA

アラゴスタ

27
H4

The name of this restaurant is Italian for "lobster" — the specialty of the chef, who trained at a hotel in Rome. Lunch set menus from ¥1,300 include pasta, dessert, and coffee. Full-course dinners from ¥4,000. The authentic cuisine draws many visiting and resident Italians.

7-3 Araki-cho, Shinjuku-ku ☎ 3358-8272 S Yotsuya-sanchome Sta. ⏰ 12:00-14:00, 17:00-23:00 H Sun. ¥ ★ ★ C DN, VISA, AMEX

CARMINE

GRANATA

グラナータ

17
E2

The chef was born in Rome but his repertory includes treats from Sicily, Bologna and the rest of Italy. The eight lunch courses usually range from ¥1,200 to ¥3,000 and full dinner courses start at ¥6,000 and contain both meat and fish. The brick and wood interior is like a bit of Italy in Japan, its cheeriness adding to the pleasure of the food. Reservations are necessary.

5-3-3 Akasaka, Minato-ku ☎ 3582-3241 S Akasaka Sta. ⏰ 11:00-21:30 H None ¥★★★ C JCB, DN, VISA, MC, AMEX

LA COMETA

LA COMETA

ラ・コメータ

16
B6

This authentic restaurant prepares a different menu of foods from all over Italy each day, depending on the season and the availability of ingredients. They have a large stock of Italian wine, and will recommend one to go with your meal in any price range you specify. Courses from ¥3,500. Among the a la carte dishes, the grilled beef (¥3,000) is a popular favorite.

1-7-2 Azabu-juban, Minato-ku ☎ 3470-5105 S Roppongi Sta. ⏰ 12:00-14:00 17:30-21:30 H Sun. ¥★★★ C DN, VISA, AMEX

TAVERNA | 27
タベルナ | E1

A casual, comfortable restaurant serving authentic Roman-style food. Choose your own antipasti from the 25 or so on display. The dinner sets, from ¥2,500, typically include antipasti, spaghetti or pizza, a choice of five main dishes, and dessert.

2-15-10 Takadanobaba, Shinjuku-ku ☎ 3232-1997 JR S Takadanobaba Sta. ◷ 17:00-23:00 H Sun. ¥ ★★ C None

IL CASTELLO | 27
イル・キャステロ | E1

Featuring mainly foods from the Tuscany region, Il Castello is a favorite for pigeon, quail, and other game birds seldom found elsewhere in Japan. Lunch menus from ¥1,500. The ¥3,800 dinner menu includes mixed antipasti, pasta, a main dish of meat or fish, dessert, and coffee.

1-34-14 Takadanobaba, Shinjuku-ku ☎ 3208-0432 JR S Takadanobaba Sta. ◷ 11:30-14:00, 17:00-23:00 H Sun. ¥ ★★ C None

IL BOCCALONE | 25
イル・ボッカローネ | H6

Specializes in Florentine, Roman, and other central Italian cuisine. A la carte menu only. Especially popular here are simple Tuscan-style meat and fish dishes, cooked over a large charcoal grill and flavored only with olive oil, salt, and pepper. Italian wine makes an excellent accompaniment.

1-15-9 Ebisu, Shibuya-ku ☎ 3449-1430 S JR Ebisu Sta. ◷ 18:00-23:00 H Sun. ¥★★★ C VISA, AMEX

TAVERNA

ATTORE	アトーレ	1-11-2 Ginza, Chuo-ku	☎3535-1111	**13・E4**
CAPITOLINO	キャピトリーノ	1-11-13 Nishi-azabu, Minato-ku	☎3479-5696	**20・C1**
MARIE	マリーエ	5-2-39 Minami-azabu, Minato-ku	☎3446-9700	**20・C3**
CHIANTI	キャンティ	3-17-26 Nishi-azabu, Minato-ku	☎3404-6500	**20・C1**
ALPORTO	アルポルト	3-24-9 Nishi-azabu, Minato-ku	☎3403-2916	**20・C1**
EL TOULA	エル・トゥーラ	5-3-10 Minami-aoyama, Minato-ku	☎3406-8831	**23・H5**
LA SCALA	ラ・スカラ	3-7 Koji-machi, Chiyoda-ku	☎3265-9191	**17・G1**
BUNRYU	文流	1-26-5 Takadanobaba, Shinjuku-ku	☎3208-5447	**27・F1**

EATING & DRINKING

EL CASTELLANO | 25
エル・カステリアーノ | H1

The ambience is relaxed and the hospitality warm at this well known Spanish restaurant, owned and operated by a native of the Galicia region. The family-style food includes home-cured ham, rabbit, gazpacho (a cold tomato soup), and paella. All go well with either sangria or Spanish wine. The Spanish-style interior has ten tables and a counter. Live flamenco guitar nightly.

2-9-11 Shibuya, Shibuya-ku ☎ 3407-7197 [S] [JR] Shibuya Sta. 🕐 18:00-23:00 [H] Sun. [¥] ★★ [C] None

EL CASTELLANO

LOS REYES MAGOS | 26
ロス・レイエス・マーゴス | B6

This Southern European-style restaurant occupies its own building on the shopping street that runs in front of Sangubashi station. The flowery tablecloths contribute to the same cheerful mood you might find at a small restaurant in the Spanish countryside. A la carte menu only; dishes include Valencia-style paella and sole meuniére Sangria by the decanter, ¥950.

5-55-7 Yoyogi, Shibuya-ku ☎ 3469-8231 [P] Oda-kyu Line Sangubashi Sta. 🕐 17:30-22:30 [H] Sun. [¥] ★★ [C] JCB, VISA, UC, MC

POCO A POCO | 22
ポコ・ア・ポコ | C1

With the jamon serrano (cured ham), chorizo, and garlic hanging from the rafters, this could be a small bar in the Spanish countryside. The food is genuine as well, with key ingredients imported from Spain. Accompany your meal with Spanish wine or a champagne spritzer made from the country's excellent sparkling wine. Recommendations include the Spanish tortillas (potato omlettes), Madrid-style beef tripe stew, and squid cooked in its own ink.

3-1-24 Jingu-mae, Shibuya-ku ☎ 3404-5888 [S] Gaien-mae Sta. 🕐 18:00-24:00 [H] Sun. & hol. [¥] ★★ [C] None

DARYE | 12
ダリエ | B3

The only place in Japan for authentic Romanian cuisine. Romanians, like other Latin races, see mealtimes as the highlight of the day. Most dishes are simple and straightforward. You'll enjoy them here to the accompaniment of recorded Romanian folk music. Lunch courses from ¥1,200. Romanian wine is available too.

7-8-5 Ginza, Chuo-ku ☎ 3573-3630 [S] Ginza Sta. 🕐 11:30-15:00, 17:00-21:30 [H] Sun. [¥] ★★ [C] JCB, DN, VISA, MC, AMEX, others

DARYE

VOLGA	17
ヴォルガ	E6

Volga's ornate egg-shaped dome makes it look less like a restaurant than a Russian Orthodox church. Inside the soft carpets and twinkling chandeliers create a truly luxurious mood. Seven different set menus are offered at lunchtime, ¥1,200 to ¥3,500. Dinner menus begin at ¥6,000, for which you receive an hors d'œuvre, soup, beef stroganoff, dessert, and Russian tea. A la carte dishes also available. The food is authentic, and ingredients are top quality. Live balalaika music.

3-5-14 Shiba-koen, Minato-ku ☎ 3433-1766 Ⓢ Kamiyacho Sta. Ⓒ 11:00-14:30, 17:00-22:00 Ⓗ None ¥ ★★★ Ⓒ JCB, DN, VISA, MC, AMEX, others

VOLGA

AU BEC FIN ESPAGNE	23
オーベックファン	F1

A quality French restaurant serving complete courses featuring Kobe beef steak. Lunch from ¥7,000; dinner from ¥14,000. All seafood served here is absolutely fresh. Reservations required.

Cl Plaza BlF 2-3-1 Kita-Aoyama, Minato-ku ☎ 3470-5596 Ⓢ Gaien-mae Sta. Ⓒ 11:30-14:00, 17:00-21:30 Ⓗ None ¥★★★★ Ⓒ JCB, DN, VISA, MC, AMEX, others

KEITEL	27
カイテル	H4

Mr. Keitel, the owner and chef, hails from Mannheim, in Germany, and has won a number of awards for his cooking. Complete courses from ¥4,500. Popular items include homemade sausages, sauerkraut, and German-style potatoes. Reservations required.

5-6-4 Shinjuku, Shinjuku-ku ☎ 3354-5057 Ⓢ Shinjuku-gyoen Sta. Ⓒ 12:00-16:00, 18:00-22:00 Ⓗ Mon. ¥★★ Ⓒ None

EATING & DRINKING

Family Restaurants

"Family restaurants" in Japan are a specific genre: large, modern chain outlets, usually located on the outskirts of town and complete with parking facilities. They offer a wide variety of dishes, mostly Western, and have photos on the menu, so language shouldn't be a problem. And yes, they're designed for the whole family, so feel free to bring even small children.

Prices are reasonable: a hamburger steak, for example, will generally be about ¥900; coffee and a piece of cake, about ¥500. The set menus, including a main dish, salad, bread, and coffee, are a good bargain and are very popular. Family restaurant chains include "**Skylark**", "**Royal Host**", "**Jonathan's**", and "**Denny's**". Menus, prices, and even the food itself are fairly similar at all.

Also popular are restaurant chains that specialize in one type of food. These include "**Volks**" for steak, "**Red Lobster**" for seafood, and "**Ringer Hut**" for *sara udon* and *champon* (noodle specialties from the Nagasaki region).

NAIR `12`
ナイル `C4`

Founded in 1950, this could be called Japan's first true Indian restaurant: the owner, cooks, and all the staff are Indian. Nair serves family-style food at reasonable prices. Recommended is the Murgi Lunch features their most popular dish, chicken curry. Indian food doesn't have to be fiery hot, and the waiters here are happy to help you order dishes as mild or hot as you like.

4-10-7 Ginza, Chuo-ku ☎ 3541-8246 Ⓢ Ginza Sta. 🕐 11:30-21:30(Sun.,hol.-20:30) Ⓗ Thur.
¥★ Ⓒ JCB, DN, VISA, MC, AMEX. others

NAIR

MAHARAO `12`
マハラオ `C1`

Another Indian restaurant where high-quality food and low prices combine to create lines outside the door both at lunch and dinner. The Tandoor Mixed Grill includes tandoori chicken, mutton curry, shish kebab, nan and rice for ¥1,174 at lunchtime, ¥1,390 in the evening. The Indian mango juice is a popular drink here.

1-1-2 Yuraku-cho, Chiyoda-ku ☎ 3580-6423 Ⓢ Hibiya Sta. 🕐 11:00-22:00 Ⓗ None ¥★

ASHOKA `12`
アショカ `B3`

"Ashoka" means "king", and Tokyo's restaurant bearing this name, appropriately enough, serves the foods of the Moghul emperors. The ¥5,000 course, for example, includes tandoori chicken, Indian-style fried fish, two different curries, and an Indian dessert made of rice and milk. You're also free to put together your own courses. Reservations required for parties of four or more.

7-9-18 Ginza, Chuo-ku ☎ 3572-2377 Ⓢ Ginza Sta. 🕐 11:30-21:30 (Sun. 12:00-19:30) Ⓗ None
¥★★ Ⓒ JCB, DN, VISA, MC, AMEX. others

MOTI `17`
モティ `F1`

The popularity of this restaurant is reflected in the lines of people waiting outside its doors at lunch and dinnertime. Moti serves authentic northern Indian dishes at extremely reasonable prices. The lunch course, for example, includes your choice of three curries and nan Indian bread for just ¥900. The mild vegetable curry is a good choice for diners new to Indian cuisine, while those who like it hot will enjoy the chicken and mutton curries.

2-14-31 Akasaka, Minato-ku ☎ 3584-6640 Ⓢ Akasaka-mitsuke Sta. 🕐 11:30-22:00 Ⓗ None
¥★★ Ⓒ JCB, DN, VISA, MC, AMEX, others

MAHARAO

THE TAJ | 17
タージ | F2

You'll know you've found The Taj
when you see the nan being baked in
the tandoor oven behind the window.
The lunch course is a bargain at
¥930; dinner courses from ¥4,500.
The furnishings, imported from
India, are a clear step up from most
of Tokyo's other Indian restaurants,
and both food and service are
equally distinguished. Reservations
recommended in the evening.

3-2-7 Akasaka, Minato-ku ☎ 3586-6606 Ⓢ
Akasaka-mitsuke Sta. 🕐 11:30-14:00, 17:30-22:
00 Ⓗ Sun.¥★★ Ⓒ JCB, DN, VISA, MC, AMEX,
others

KUSA NO IE | 16
草の家 | B6

This Korean country restaurant is
frequented by employees of the nearby Korean embassy. Courses start at
¥3,800 and include kimche, seafood
salad, salted tongue and meat. If
you're ordering a la carte try the
Green Onion Pancake. Low prices
keep the tables full.

4-6-7 Azabu-juban, Minato-ku ☎ 3455-8356 Ⓢ
Mita Sta. 🕐 11:30-14:30, 17:00-23:00 Ⓗ 1st
Mon.¥★★ Ⓒ JCB, DN, VISA, MC, AMEX, others

KUSA NO IE

MAHARANA

MAHARANA | 25
マハラナ | E4

A convenient restaurant for favorite
Indian dishes. The ¥1,260 Tandoor
Mixed Grill includes tandoor
chicken, curry, shish kebab, nan, and
rice. The Full Course, for ¥2,500,
offers an even bigger selection.
Recommended for after your meal is
the Laci, a cold yoghurt drink.
Located on the 10th floor of the 109
Building.

2-29-1 Dogenzaka, Shibuya-ku ☎ 3477-5188 Ⓢ
ⒿⓇ Shibuya Sta. 🕐 11:00-21:30 Ⓗ None ¥★★
Ⓒ JCB, DN, VISA, MC, AMEX, others

MUGYODON | 17
武橋洞 | F3

This unassuming restaurant serves
good family-style Korean dishes.
The seasonings, imported directly
from Korea, make for authentic and
distinctive food. The menu is a la
carte only, but the staff can suggest
a complete meal to suit your budget,
featuring grilled meats and stews of
seasonal ingredients. Reserve for
large groups.

2-17-74 Akasaka, Minato-ku ☎ 3586-6478 Ⓢ
Akasaka Sta. 🕐 17:00-23:00 Ⓗ Sun.& hol. ¥★
Ⓒ None

BENGAWAN SOLO | 16

ブンガワン・ソロ | B5

The menu here covers a wide selection of dishes from throughout the Indonesian archipelago. Chilies are used in many of the foods, making beer the drink of choice. Complete courses from ¥9,500 for two. Recommended a la carte items include chicken satay, shrimp in coconut cream, and spicy beef.

7-18-13 Roppongi, Minato-ku ☎ 3408-5698 [S] Roppongi Sta. ⊙ 11:30-15:00 17:00-23:00 [H] None ¥★★ [C] JCB, DN, VISA, MC, AMEX, others

ROSE DE SAHARA | 27

ローズ・ド・サハラ | E4

A rarity in Japan — a restaurant specializing in African cuisine. The three different set menus offer, for example, salad, rice pilaf, shish-kebab, and dessert, from ¥3,500. Other authentic African dishes include guinea fowl in orange sauce and North African couscous (¥5,000 for two). African music too.

2-10-10 Yoyogi, Shibuya-ku ☎ 3379-6427 [S] [JR] Shinjuku Sta. ⊙ 17:00- 23:30 [H] None ¥ ★★ [C] JCB, DN, VISA, MC, AMEX, others

LA MARIMBA | 16

ラ・マリンバ | C6

Most of the ingredients are imported at this authentic Mexican restaurant. The ¥2,200 menu is designed for those with lighter appetites, while the ¥3,500 menu features some of Mexico's best known dishes: nachos, tacos, and chorizo sausage. Tequila is the natural drink of choice. The interior furnishings, all from Mexico, contribute to the atmosphere.

6-8-28 Roppongi, Minato-ku ☎ 3405-6007 [S] Roppongi Sta. ⊙ 17:00- 24:00 [H] None ¥ ★ ★ [C] JCB, DN, VISA, MC, AMEX, others

TOMOCA | 27

トモカ | H5

Sri Lankan food resembles Indian, though generally a little simpler, and no pork is used. Tomoca offers set menus only; eight dishes, for example, for ¥3,600. Drinks include Sri Lankan beer, liquor, and — naturally — the island's own tea.

1-7-27 Yotsuya, Shinjuku-ku ☎ 3353-7945 [S] Yotsuya-sanchome Sta. ⊙ 18:00-21:00 [H] Sun. & hol. ¥ ★★ [C] None

BENGAWAN SOLO

LA CASITA | 25

ラ・カシータ | G6

From the charming brick exterior to the ambience inside and the flavors of the food, this is a bit of Mexico transported to Tokyo. Much of the food is quite spicy, but they can prepare milder dishes if you ask. Try the tacos and the steak, accompanied by Mexican beer, margaritas, or shots of tequila.

13-4 Daikanyama, Shibuya-ku ☎ 3496-1850 [P] Tokyu-Toyoko Line Daikanyama Sta. ⊙ 11:00-22:00 [H] Wed. ¥ ★★ [C] None

ANGKOR WAT 22
アンコールワット | A2

Run by a Cambodian family from Phnom Penh, this restaurant offers a chance to try Cambodian family-style dishes like shrimp spring rolls and homemade sausage. Courses from a very reasonable ¥1,000, while the a la carte menu features a wide variety of rice and noodle dishes.

1-38-13 Yoyogi, Shibuya-ku ☎ 3370-3019 JR Yoyogi Sta. ⏰ 11:00-14:00 17:00-22:00 (Sun. & hol. evenings only) H None ¥★ C None

PATTAYA 24
パタヤ | B5

The shrimp, crab and other Thai-style seafood dishes here have gained an enthusiastic following among Tokyo's Thai community. Recommended is the ¥5,000 set menu, including Thai-style *sukiyaki* and coconut ice cream. Lunchtime bargains include Thai curries, rice noodles, and other dishes in the ¥800-900 price range.

1-28-8 Shoto, Shibuya-ku ☎ 3770-8777 S JR Shibuya Sta. ⏰ 17:00-23:00 H Wed. ¥ ★★ C JCB, VISA, UC.

BOUGAINVILLEA 24
ブーゲンビレア | C4

The food of Vietnam — typically wrapped in lettuce, flavored with mint leaves, and salted with fish sauce — is both flavorful and healthy. Bougainvillea features a good selection of Vietnamese dishes, mostly from the south. The ¥3,000 set menu is a fine introduction to this cuisine, and should satisfy even a hearty appetite.

2-25-9 Dogenzaka, Shibuya-ku ☎ 3496-5537 S JR Shibuya Sta. ⏰ 17:00-23:00 (Sat. Sun. & hol. 11:30-15:00, 17: 00-23:00) H Mon. ¥ ★★ C AMEX

AODAI 17
アオザイ | E3

Vietnamese cuisine uses all kinds of meat, fish, and vegetables, and — especially the South Vietnamese style cooking served here — is generally light and healthy. Courses from ¥3,500. Drinks include Thai beer and Vietnamese liquor. A popular place, so reservations are recommended.

5-4-14 Akasaka, Minato-ku ☎ 3583-0234 S Akasaka Sta. ⏰ 17:00-22:30 H Sun.& hol. ¥★★ C JCB, DN, VISA, MC, AMEX, others

ANGKOR WAT

BAN THAI 27
バンタイ | E1

The secret of the authentic flavors at Ban Thai is in the spices, imported directly from Thailand. Hot and addictive, Thai food can be sampled here a la carte or in five different set menus from ¥3,500. All include favorite dishes like tom yam kung, a fiery seafood soup, and salad.

1-23-14 Kabuki-cho, Shinjuku-ku ☎ 3207-0068 S JR Shinjuku Sta. ⏰ 17:00-4:00(Mon-24:00) H None ¥ ★★ C None

A LECOMTE	16
ル・コント	B5

French people often visit this cake shop for the authentic flavor only a French chef could create. Popular treats are the mont blanc (¥500), mille feuille and fraisse (¥400).

16 Fuji Bldg. 7-18-12 Roppongi, Minato-ku ☎ 3402-5991 [S] Roppongi Sta. ⏰ 10:30-22:00 [H] Sun. [¥]★ [C] None

A LECOMTE

AOYAMA CHANDON	25
青山シャンドン	H2

A small yet elegant cake shop. The cakes (about ¥280) are made with only the best butter for rich flavor. Home-made cookies and chocolate are also sold and these are as popular as the cake. If you're not in the mood for sweets try one of their fluffy omelets.

2-9-2 Shibuya, Shibuya-ku ☎ 3400-8198 [S] [JR] Shibuya Sta. [S] Omote-sando Sta. ⏰ 10:00-20:00 (Sun. & hol. 10:00-19:30) [H] None [¥]★ [C] None

BAMBOO COURT	24
バンブーコート	D2

When you're strolling around Shibuya and suddenly struck by the desire to eat something delicious, turn off Koen-dori street to the Juni-kagetsu Building. Although slightly expensive, these are top quality restaurants with good food. If you're in the mood for cake, try this shop on the first floor — mille feuille at ¥450 is especially popular. The choux pastry is lined with seasonal fruit and sherbet for a result that is pleasing to both the eye and the palate.

Junikagetsu Bldg. 1-18-7 Jinnan, Shibuya-ku ☎ 3464-8647 [S] [JR] Shibuya Sta. ⏰ 11:00-23:30 [H] None [¥]★ [C] JCB, DN, VISA, MC, AMEX

AOYAMA CHANDON

SEIRONTEI	—
青論亭	—

Our recommendation is the seasonal fruitcake (¥300-350) made with bananas, walnuts and other goodies. All the standards like chocolate layer cake are available too. Enjoy one of the ten different kinds of tea with your cake.

Shingakai Bldg. 2F 1-14-12 Kami-Ogi, Suginami-ku ☎ 3398-2352 [S] [JR] Ogikubo Sta. ⏰ 11:00-21:30 [H] None [¥]★ [C] None

ALMOND (Roppongi Branch) 16
アマンド | C5

The interior of this tea room is coordinated with a pleasant pink. It also serves as a landmark for meeting people in Roppongi. Try the short cake (¥360) and cream puffs (¥200). There are sister shops all over Tokyo where you can enjoy the same high quality.

6-1-26 Roppongi, Minato-ku ☎ 3402-1800 ⓈRoppongi Sta. 🕐 9:00-5:00(Mon.-Thu.),-6:00(Fri., Sat.),-3:00(Sun.,hol.) Ⓗ None ¥ ★ Ⓒ None

HAAGEN DAZS

GLACIERIE CHEZ LUI 25
シェ・リュイ | G6

This ice cream shop is sister to the famous French restaurant in Daikanyama, Chez Lui. Many unusual flavors like pumpkin, tea and cheese are offered. In the summer it is always crowded with co-eds from the nearby college. Attractive ice cream cakes (¥260-300) are also available.

4-8-30 Kudan-Minami, Chiyoda-ku ☎ 3239-7964 Ⓢ JⓇ Ichigaya Sta. 🕐 9:00-22:00 Ⓗ None ¥ ★ Ⓒ None

COZY CORNER (Akasaka Branch) 17
コージーコーナー | F1

When hearing this name, the first thing that usually comes to mind is cream puffs (¥100 each) and an original confection called oreyu (¥120). Of course they have petit fours (¥120), short cake (about ¥300) and many other kinds of cakes too. Branches can be found all over the city. Reasonable prices mean you don't need a special occasion to eat cake.

Kinpar Bldg. 1F 2-14-31 Akasaka, Minato-ku ☎ 3585-7017 Ⓢ Akasaka-mitsuke Sta. 🕐 9:00-23:00 (Sun. & hol. -22:00) Ⓗ None ¥ ★ Ⓒ None

HÄAGEN DAZS 23
ハーゲンダッツ | F3

This store is famous for the 100% natural ice cream that it serves. Branches can be found in Harajuku and Yokohama too. No matter which one you visit they're all full of young people and expatriates. Our recommendation is the Danish cone with whipped cream and chocolate topping (¥370).

Plaza 246 Bldg. 3-1-1 Minami-Aoyama, Minato-ku ☎3404-5513 Ⓢ Gaien-mae Sta. 🕐 11:00-23:00 (Sun. -22:30) Ⓗ None ¥ ★ Ⓒ None

ITALIAN GELATO —
イタリアンジェラート | —

The leading Italian ice cream shop. Low fat ingredients are used to keep it healthy. Fresh fruits are made into delicious ice cream flavors like apple and kiwi. Each day about 30 flavors are arrayed from a selection of over a hundred.

Tamagawa Takashimaya Bldg. B1F 3-17-1 Tamagawa, Setagaya-ku ☎ 3709-3111 Ⓟ Tokyu Shin-Tamagawa Line Futako-Tamagawa Sta. 🕐 10:00-19:00 Ⓗ Wed. ¥ ★ Ⓒ None

UMEMURA | 32
梅むら | C3

The specialty of this traditional confectionery is *mamekan* (¥350). This is an ancient delicacy consisting of cubes of agar agar and boiled peas covered with brown sugar syrup. Relax here after visiting Sensoji Temple.

3-22-12 Asakusa, Taito-ku ☎ 3873-6992 [S] Asakusa Sta. ⏲ 13:00-22:00 [H] Sun.[¥]★ [C] None

IZUMIYA | 16
和泉屋 | A5

This traditional and western confectionery is famous as the first to produce sweet potatoes in Japan. In the adjoining confectionery, Japanese sweets and green tea sets can be enjoyed for ¥600. The *kuzumochi* (kudzu starch sweet) and *tokoroten* (agar-agar in vinegar and soy sauce) are also delicious.

1-7-5 Nishi-Azabu, Minato-ku ☎ 3404-8811 [S] Shiba-Koen Sta. ⏲ 9:00-21:00 [H] None[¥]★ [C] JCB, DN, VISA,MC, AMEX, others

YANAGIBASHI-NINKIYA

YANAGIBASHI-NINKIYA | 32
柳橋にんきや | A2

Long a popular place to satisfy sweet tooths, everything is delicious but the *anmitsu* (bean jam, agar agar and fruit in syrup, ¥420) is especially recommended. In the winter, the *shiruko* (sweet bean soups) are also good.

1-3-12 Yanagibashi, Taito-ku ☎ 3851-1002 [S] [JR] Asakusa-bashi Sta. ⏲ 11:30-20:00 (Sat. -18:00) [H] Sun. & hol.[¥]★ [C] None

KAMON | 26
香門 | A2

Although located in the ultra-modern Hilton International Building, this purely Japanese sweet shop has a totally traditional interior. A traditional sweet with one of the many kinds of teas runs from ¥650-1,200. The tea comes in a large pot filled with hot water so you can drink as many cups as you want at your own pace.

Tokyo Hilton International Bldg. B1F 6-6-2 Nishi-Shinjuku, Shinjuku-ku☎ 3348-2556 [S] [JR] Shinjuku Sta.⏲ 10:00-20:00 [H] None[¥]★ [C] None

TAKEMURA | 29
竹むら | G4

This traditional sweet shop was founded in 1930. Cherry blossom tea is provided as a service at the tables. The most popular treat here is definitely the *age-manju* (deep-fried buns). The crispy thin crust is filled with mildly sweetened bean paste. Amazingly enough, although fried, they remain light. They are best when fresh-fried and hot so eat them there instead of taking them home.

1-19 Kanda-Sudacho, Chiyoda-ku ☎ 3251-2328 [S] [JR] Kanda Sta. ⏲ 11:00-20:00 [H] Sun. & hol.[¥]★ [C] None

KOTOTOI DANGO | 32
言問団子 | C6

When the first owner opened this shop at the end of the Edo period, he took the name from a poem by Narihira Ariwara. The fine *dango* (flavored pounded rice balls on a stick) have pleased palates for more than a hundred and fifty years. Three different kinds of bean paste, white, red and green are wrapped around the balls and served on an elegant plate (¥420).

5-5-22 Mukojima, Sumida-ku ☎ 3622-0081 Ⓢ Hikifune Sta. ◷ 10:00-18:00 Ⓗ Thur. ¥ ★ Ⓒ None

WAKABA

HABUTAE DANGO | 31
羽二重団子 | C1

Dealing only in *dango* since it opened its doors in 1819, the name of this shop has appeared in works by famous authors like Soseki Natsume and Kyoka Izumi. A skewer of soy-sauce flavored balls and one coated with sweetened bean paste can be had as a set for ¥360. The perfect place to experience the *shitamachi*, or downtown, atmosphere of the Edo period.

5-54-3 Higashi-Nippori, Arakawa-ku ☎ 3891-2924 Ⓢ 🚉 Nippori Sta. ◷ 9:00-17:30 Ⓗ Tue. ¥ ★ Ⓒ None

WAKABA | 27
わかば | H4

Named after its location, the star of this shop is the *taiyaki* (¥100). A thin cake in the shape of a fish is filled from head to tail with sweetened bean paste. They're not too sweet so you'll want more than one!

1-10 Wakaba, Shinjuku-ku ☎ 3351-4396 Ⓢ 🚉 Yotsuya Sta. ◷ 9:00-19:00 Ⓗ Sun. ¥ ★ Ⓒ None

YANAGIYA | 19
柳屋 | F6

People line up for the delicious *taiyaki* (¥90 each). The ice cream (¥100) is also good so try that too if you're eating there. The traditional downtown atmosphere will add to your enjoyment.

2-11-3 Nihonbashi Ningyo-cho Chuo-ku ☎ 3666-9901 Ⓢ Ningyo-cho Sta. ◷ 10:30-19:00 (hol. -18:00) Ⓗ Sun. ¥ ★ Ⓒ None

KIMURAYA SOHONTEN | 12
木村屋総本店 | D3

The inventor of that popular treat, *anpan*, or bread stuffed with sweet bean paste. Founded in 1869, *anpan* was developed in 1875 and still serves as the Kimuraya trademark today. At the tea room on the second floor an *anpan* set can be had for ¥600. The flavor of freshly made *anpan* is not to missed.

4-5-7 Ginza, Chuo-ku ☎ 3561-0091 Ⓢ Ginza Sta. ◷ 10:00-21:00 (tea room: 11:00-20:30) Ⓗ None ¥ ★ Ⓒ None

KIMURAYA SOHONTEN

EATING & DRINKING

Beer Under the Stars: Tokyo's Beer Gardens

Elsewhere in these pages we talk about beer halls, both long-established, big German-style cellars like Lion and Pilsen, and the newer, more fashionable places set up by beer makers. But beer lovers in Japan have another interesting choice: outdoor beer gardens.

Most of Tokyo's beer gardens are to be found on the roofs of the city's department stores. Owing to the climate, they generally operate only in the summer, which is to say about four months a year. An evening at any one of them, under the stars of (we hope) a clear summer sky, is an experience that no indoor beer hall can match. Seldom does a cold mug of beer taste so good — or so easily lead to another.

SUPER DRY HALL	32
スーパードライホール	A4

A strange golden object rises out of the nightscape around the Sumida River. The first and second floor of the building under the object is a beer hall. Both the object and the building, inside and out, are the work of French designer Philippe Starck. Most of the food is French but fried jumbo shrimp (¥1300) is one of the most popular dishes.
1-23-1 Azumabashi, Sumida-ku ☎ 5608-5381 ⓢ Asakusa Sta. ⓣ 11:30-22:00 Ⓗ None ¥★★ Ⓒ JCB, DN, VISA, MC, AMEX

SUPER DRY HALL

KIRIN CITY	27
キリンシティ	F3

The news of this new, European-style beer hall spread through Tokyo like wildfire. The sounds of voices and glasses clinking pull you in like a magnet. The most popular side-dish is a sausage platter (¥580). Lunch is served from 11:30-14:00.
Shinjuku-kurihashi Bldg. 2F 3-15 Shinjuku, Shinjuku-ku ☎ 3226-8230 ⓢ ⒥ⓡ Shinjuku Sta. ⓣ 11:00-23:00 Ⓗ None ¥★★ Ⓒ None

PILSEN	12
ピルゼン	C3

A valiant attempt to recreate an authentic European beer hall, this has long been a favorite place to stop on the way home from work. Its location provides a glimpse of the Ginza of bygone days. The food is all delicious and inexpensive, with Eastern European specialities like sauerkraut (¥780) and frankfurters (¥400).
Kojunsha Bldg. 1F 6-8-7 Ginza, Chuo-ku ☎ 3571-3443 ⓢ Ginza Sta. ⓣ 12:00-22:00 (Sun. & hol. -21:00) Ⓗ None ¥★ Ⓒ JCB, VISA, MC, AMEX

LION	12
ライオン	B3

The unassuming atmosphere of this beer hall has kept it in business for a long time. All the food compliments the beer but the specialities are veal in cream sauce (¥1,280) and spaghetti with fresh tomatoes (¥950). The trademark high ceiling and brick walls can be found in sister shops all over the city too. A good place to share a few with your friends.

7-9-20 Ginza, Chuo-ku ☎ 3571-2590 S Ginza Sta. S JR Shinbashi Sta. ⏰ 1F 11:30-22:30 2F 11:30-22:30 H None ¥★★ C JCB, DN, VISA, MC, AMEX, others

WINDS	17
ウィンズ	F2

A popular spot among beer lovers, the side dishes are inexpensive and delicious and it is one of the few places with Budweiser on tap in Tokyo. A signboard showing the ideal temperature which beer should be consumed at for the day stands in front.

Akasaka Gessekai Bldg. 1F 3-10-4 Akasaka, Minato-ku ☎ 3582-8951 S Akasaka-mitsuke Sta. ⏰ 17:00-2:00 H Sun. & hol. ¥★★ C JCB, DN, VISA, MC, AMEX, others

STRATHISLA	12
ストラスアイラ	D4

The first floor is quite chic while B1F is more sedate. You can enjoy a relaxed whiskey accompanied the cuisine of Alsace. The chef's recommended hors d'œuvre are from ¥1,800. The whiskey is a Strathisla exclusive.

Yonei Bldg. 1F, B1F 2-8-20 Ginza, Chuo-ku ☎ 3535-3118 S Ginza-1chome Sta. ⏰ 1F 11:30-23:00, B1F 17:30-23:00 H None ¥★★ C JCB, DN, VISA, MC, AMEX, others

HOFBRÄUHAUS MÜNCHEN IN TOKYO	27
ホフブロイハウス	F3

Not only is the beer directly imported in kegs from Germany, some of the waitress are even German in this branch of the famous Munich beer hall. Some of the authentic specialities created by the German chef include the sausage platter (¥1,500) and omelets (¥900). Course menus are also available.

Meiji Seimei Shinjuku-Higashi Bldg. B1F 1-1-17 Kabuki-cho, Shinjuku-ku ☎ 3207-7591 P Seibu-Shinjuku Line Seibu-Shinjuku Sta. ⏰ 17:30-23:30 (Sat., Sun., & hol. 15:00-23:30) H None ¥★★ C JCB, DN, VISA, MC, AMEX, others

LION

K'S BAR	25
ケーズ バー	H2

Although a bar in the western sense, all the food served is Japanese. It is an excellent place to enjoy a leisurely drink. If the weather is good, you can relax on the terrace in front. Favorite items on the menu include *daikon* salad (¥800) and potato croquets (¥900).

St. Aoyama Bldg. 1F 2-6-8 Shibuya, Shibuya-ku ☎ 3400-8885 S JR Shibuya Sta. ⏰ 19:00-2:00 (Sun. & hol. 18:00-24:00) H None ¥★★ C None

EATING & DRINKING

105

LEXINGTON QUEEN	16
レキシントンクィーン	C5

A disco-bar located just a stone's throw from the well known discos of Roppongi's Square Bldg. The decor here sets a stylish mood, and the clientele includes many foreign entertainers visiting Japan. Non-Japanese speakers can telephone in advance to be met by English-speaking staff.

Daisan Goto Bldg. B1F 3-13-14 Roppongi, Minato-ku ☎ 3401-1661 ⓢ Roppongi Sta. ⏰ 18:00-24:00 Ⓗ None ¥ Men 4,000 Women 3,000 Ⓒ JCB, DN, VISA, MC, AMEX, others

J TRIP BAR END MAX	16
ジェイ・トリップ・バー・エンド・マックス	D5

Renowned for the interior designed by popular artist Katsuhiko Hibino. The S-shaped stairway has become familiar to everyone. The food is all good but if you're hungry you might try the popular original beef curry (¥900).

3-4-18 Roppongi, Minato-ku ☎ 3586-0639 ⓢ Roppongi Sta. ⏰ 18:00-Midnight Ⓗ None ¥★★ Ⓒ JCB, DN, VISA, MC, AMEX, others

KAMIYA BAR	32
神谷バー	B3

Renowned as the oldest bar in Japan, it is located right near a Kaminarimon Gate in front of Sensoji Temple. People come here to drink the famous Kamiya original, a sweet cocktail called *Denki Bran* (60 proof:¥230, 80 proof: ¥350) made with a brandy base. The food here is good too.

1-1-1 Asakusa, Taito-ku ☎ 3841-5400 ⓢ Asakusa Sta. Ⓟ Tobu-Isesaki Line Asakusa Sta. ⏰ 11:30-22:00 Ⓗ Tue. ¥★★ Ⓒ None

KOHAKU	31
琥珀	B5

One of the oldest bars in the Ueno area. The bar is well stocked and almost any drink can be mixed. Its age has been no barrier to adding the newest innovations.

3-44-1 Yushima, Bunkyo-ku ☎ 3831-3913 ⓢ Yushima Sta. ⏰ 18:00-23:45 Ⓗ Sun. & hol. ¥★★ Ⓒ None

KAMIYA BAR

BILLBOARD	24
ビルボード	D4

The strains of the billboard top one hundred fill the bar. It is frequented by DJ's and other people in the business but the staff is friendly and helpful.

Ejima Bldg. B1F 25-1 Udagawa-cho, Shibuya-ku ☎ 3464-9208 ⓢ ⒿⓇ Shibuya Sta. ⏰ 11:00-23:30 (Fri. & Sat. -1:00) Ⓗ None ¥★ Ⓒ None

EDO-ICHI

EDO-ICHI	30
江戸一	D6

Only the best kinds of *sake* are offered here which is natural as Edo-ichi was once a *sake* store. Enjoy the inexpensive and delicious snacks with your *sake* on the white wood counter. We recommend the fish, especially the *sashimi* and short-neck clams steamed in *sake*.
2-45-4 Minami-Otsuka, Toshima-ku ☎ 3945-3032 JR Otsuka Sta. ◷ 17:00-22:00 H Sun. & hol. ¥ ★ C None

KUREMUTSU	32
暮六つ	B3

A lively *shitamachi* (downtown) tavern. The cook is confident in his skill but *kabutoni* (¥5,000), sea bream heads boiled with soy sauce, is a specialty. Instead of rice, more unusual offerings like tea-buckwheat noodles are provided. The interior is pleasantly old-fashioned.
2-2-13 Asakusa, Taito-ku ☎ 3842-0906 S Tawaramachi Sta. ◷ 16:00-22:00 H Thur. ¥★ ★★ C None

ISETO	–
伊勢藤	–

A braided rope curtain marks the entrance to this interesting bar. It is not a place to drink noisily, but rather to savor the taste of fine *sake* (¥450). The cook works hard preparing side dishes that will compliment the flavor of this Japanese wine. Language will not be a problem here.
4-2 Kagurazaka, Shinjuku-ku ☎ 3260-6363 S Kagurazaka Sta. S JR Iidabashi Sta. ◷ 17:00-21:30 H Sun. & hol. ¥ C None

KUREMUTSU

KANEDA	–
金田	–

There are about eighty items on the menu to choose from! The seasonal home-style dishes are affordable at ¥300-1,500. Lightly seasoned, they go well with *sake*. Enjoy them at tables or in private rooms.
1-11-4 Jiyugaoka, Meguro-ku ☎ 3717-7352 P Tokyu-Toyoko Line Jiyugaoka Sta. ◷ 17:00-22:00 H Sun. ¥★ C None

EATING & DRINKING

SUMIYA 16

炭屋 D5

Although Roppongi brings to mind discos, there are some quiet spots like this traditional one. The specialty is *kushiyaki* (food grilled on skewers) and courses are available (¥3,600-6,800). The seafood is especially good. The simple, sedate interior appeals to all ages.

Coco Bldg. 6F 3-11-10 Roppongi, Minato-ku
☎ 3403-5559 S Roppongi Sta. ⏰ 17:30-1:00 (hol. -24:00) H Sun. ¥★★ C JCB, DN, VISA, MC, AMEX, others

BORUGA

TOTOYA 27

ととや H3

Cheap and delicious. The food is generally traditional home style and it is as popular among expatriates as it is the natives. The counter is a no-smoking area, quite rare in Japan. We recommend the grilled fish and boiled dishes.

7 Arakicho, Shinjuku-ku ☎ 3357-3319 S Yotsuya-sanchome Sta. ⏰ 17:30-21:00 H Sun. & hol. ¥★ C None

BORUGA 26

ぼるが D2

Smoke from the *yakitori* (grilled chicken) wafts from this old brick tavern. The walls carpeted with ivy are an impressive sight. It is a good place to relax which brings many regular customers every night. At ¥80 per skewer for *yakitori*, the prices are certainly affordable. Take out is available too.

1-4-18 Nishi-Shinjuku, Shinjuku-ku ☎ 3342-4996 S JR Shinjuku Sta. ⏰ 17:00-23:00 H Sun. & hol. ¥★ C None

NEZU NO JINPACHI 31

根津の甚八 A3

The owner is exceptionally cheerful and pleasant. He runs the place himself so if you can speak a little Japanese, stop by and enjoy some interesting conversation with him. Located in the traditional downtown area where you can get a whiff of the past.

2-26-4 Nezu, Bunkyo-ku ☎ 3823-1309 S Nezu Sta. ⏰ 17:00-21:30 H None ¥★★ C None

NAKAGAWA 12

中川 B1

A Tokyo home-style restaurant set amid a cluster of office buildings. Fresh fish are stocked every day so prices vary but you can usually enjoy something delicious for ¥800-1,200. A tasty fresh fish lunch is only ¥600 which brings crowds of workers from nearby offices.

1-14-8 Nishi-Shinbashi, Minato-ku ☎ 3591-2976 S Uchisaiwaicho Sta. ⏰ 11:30-13:30, 17:00-21:00 H Sat., Sun. & hol. ¥★ C None

SANGYODO | 25

三漁洞 | F5

Marked by three cute little red fish, one can easily guess that seafood is served here but it is prepared in an original manner. Crab and scallop grilled with corn, short-necked clams steamed with *sake*, boiled, fried, the menu covers a wide range. *Chinmi*, the sort of things we usually throw away although considered delicacies by some, are also available for the brave. The interior was patterned after a theater. *Zashiki* are available.

Brian Shibuya Bldg. B1F 2-1 Sakuragaoka, Shibuya-ku ☎ 3496-3905 Ⓢ ⒿⓇ Shibuya Sta. 🕐 17:00-23:00 🄷 Sun. & hol. ¥ ★★ Ⓒ DN, VISA, AMEX

ICHIMON | 32

一文 | C2

This tavern is unique even in Tokyo. The name is taken from a coin that has long been out of circulation. It is run on an unusual system where you are handed a wooden tag corresponding to a certain amount and when you leave, your eating and drinking expenses are deducted and the remainder returned. The food is generally light and the *Takebue tofu*, *tofu* run through a bamboo tube, is popular in the summer.

3-12-6 Asakusa, Taito-ku ☎ 3875-6800 Ⓢ Iriya Sta. 🕐 17:00-23:00 🄷 Sun. & hol. ¥ ★ Ⓒ AMEX

IZAKAYA

There are times when you want a quiet drink in a fashionable bar or pub but there are also times when you want to enjoy boisterous conversation in a more relaxed atmosphere. For the latter, the best place in Japan is an *izakaya*, or tavern. The many chains are quite inexpensive so you can safely eat and drink to your heart's content. Some of the most well-known are: Tsubohachi, Shoya, Kita no Kazoku, Penguin's Bar, Murasaki, Suzume no Oyado, and Tengu. The interiors are plain and neat as the sales point is price. Snacks run about ¥200-600 and a large bottle of beer is ¥410. The menus consist mainly of plain Japanese food like *nikujaga* (meat and potatoes), *yakitori*, and *sashimi* but salad and pizza can also be found as much of their clientele students and other young people. The energetic, cheerful atmosphere is not only a place to enjoy old friendships but a place to make new ones too.

Eating Cheaply in Tokyo

Food in Tokyo is generally expensive, but that doesn't mean you can't eat cheaply. One popular way to do so is at the simple restaurant stands found around the city, especially near railway stations. While a single bowl of noodles at one of these shops may or may not fill you up, it certainly won't empty your wallet. Typically a bowl of *tempura soba* will be about ¥200; a bowl of "curry rice," about ¥400. Next are the outdoor stalls usually found around entertainment districts at night. Ramen noodles are typical of the fare served here, at a price of about ¥500 per bowl. If you're looking for large portions of nutritious food at economical prices, university cafeterias are worth knowing about. All universities allow the general public to eat at their cafeterias, which typically offer a wide selection of foods like *ramen*, *soba*, spaghetti, and *teishoku* meal sets. And they're invariably cheap. At Meiji University's cafeteria in Ochanomizu, for example, you can have "curry rice" for ¥240, or a meal of cheese cutlet, rice and *miso* soup for just ¥350. Moreover these places offer a glimpse into ordinary Japanese life that you won't see by simply walking around the streets. Many coffeehouses offer an inexpensive (¥300-400) breakfast of toast, salad, coffee, etc., for the first few hours they're open each day. Many restaurants likewise advertise a lunchtime special (*teishoku*) from about 11 am. to 2 pm. These usually run from ¥600 to ¥1,000, which is quite a bargain, since they include almost as much food as the restaurant would serve for dinner. But note that restaurants serving cheap lunches tend to be crowded, and a meal at one of these places is seldom a leisurely proposition.

SHOPPING

Famous brand names or the simplest handmade crafts....
Here's what to buy and where to find it.

Where to Shop

The high prices of Tokyo are by now almost legendary. That's the bad news. The good news is that the shops of Japan's capital reflect the remarkable economic prosperity of the nation. Anything and everything is available here, and any one of Tokyo's main shopping districts offers a staggering selection of goods. Most famous of those districts is the Ginza. The atmosphere here is decidedly upmarket: a wide thoroughfare lined with elegant shops —— many of which have been in business for decades —— offering adult fashions and other luxury goods. Ginza and the neighboring area of Yurakucho are also home to almost a dozen major department stores. For younger fashions, the names to know are Aoyama and Harajuku. Many of Japan's leading contemporary designers are based here, and their boutiques offer the latest styles. Ikebukuro, Shinjuku, and Shibuya are all stops on the circular Yamanote train line. All are dominated by large department stores and sprawling shopping districts. The mood is more down-to-earth than Ginza, and the shopping more relaxed. Shibuya, with its many fashion buildings, is a particular favorite among young people. In contrast with all these areas are Asakusa and Nihonbashi with their many older, more Japanese-style shops. Either one is excellent for local handicrafts and other traditional items. Tokyo also has many specialized shopping areas —— neighborhoods known for one specific type of item, like cookware, or toys, or electrical appliances. We include a number of these in our listings.

Shopping Questions and Answers

Unless you speak Japanese, your immediate concern with shopping in Japan will probably be language: will you be able to communicate? English is relatively widely understood in Tokyo —— but only in comparison to the rest of the country. English-speaking sales personnel are still the exception rather than the rule. If you need detailed explanations, stick to large department stores or shops that actively solicit foreign customers. The next question is likely to about prices. Are they negotiable? The answer is yes and no. Some shops will discount from a marked price, while others won't. Fixed prices are the rule at all department stores and supermarkets. Most small retailers in principle will not bargain over prices, but some might negotiate in certain cases. Bargaining is very much the name of the game in the electronics shops of Akihabara. You should also be able to obtain discounts in markets like Tsukiji and Ameyoko. How about credit cards? Many shops in Japan now accept them, though older, more traditional, and smaller retailers often will not. Be sure to check before they start ringing up your purchases. Finally, is there any danger walking around with cash and credit cards? Japan remains a very safe country, and pickpockets are extremely rare. But in Tokyo, as in any big city, it pays to maintain at least a little vigilance.

The name Akihabara has by now become synonymous worldwide with electronic goods at bargain prices. The streets of this area are filled with the gaudy fluorescent signs of more than 400 electronics shops. Some buildings contain dozens of small shops, while some of the bigger stores each range over a number of buildings. All offer big discounts and reliable after-sales service. The main stores, handling a complete range of items, include names like Ishimaru Denki, Minami Denki, Sato Musen, and Yamagiwa. And the wares themselves? Naturally you'll find audio equipment, including the latest CD units, as well as televisions and VTRs and videos to play on them. But there is much more, from

computers to state-of-the-art electronic components. The trick to getting the best price is to ask around at a number of shops. Then when you find the shop quoting the lowest figure, bargain them down even further. You should always be able to get at least a small additional discount from the posted price.

Ueno, Taito-ku [S] [JR] Akihabara Sta. ⏰ Hours vary; usually 10:00-19:00 [H] Most shops are open every day

AKIHABARA ELECTRICAL GOODS DISTRICT

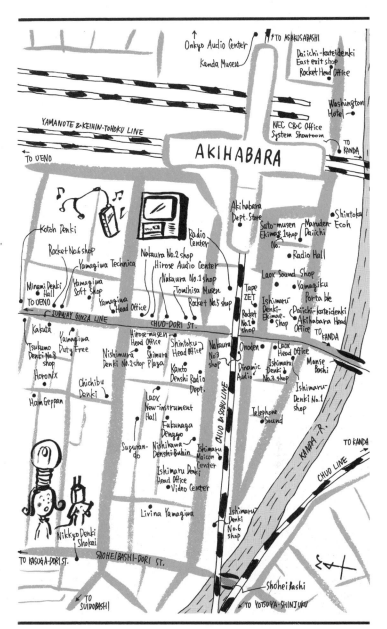

Onkyo Audio Center
Kanda Musen
↑↑TO ASAKUSABASHI
Daiichi-kateidenki
East exit shop
Rocket Head Office
Washington Hotel •
NEC C&C Office
System Showroom
TO KANDA
YAMANOTE & KEIHIN-TOHOKU LINE
AKIHABARA
← TO UENO
Akihabara Dept. Store
Sato-musen Ekimae 1 shop No. •
Shintoku
Maruden-Ecoh
Daiichi
Kotoh Denki
Radio Center
• Radio Hall
Rocket No.6 shop
Yamagiwa Technica
Nakaura No.2 shop
Hirose Audio Center
Nakaura No.1 shop
Tomihisa Musen
Rocket No.5 shop
Laox Sound Shop
Yamagiku
Porta ble
Minami Denki Hall •
Yamagiwa Soft Shop
Yamagiwa Head Office
Tape ZET
Rocket No.1 shop
Ishimaru Denki-Ekimae- Shop
Daiichi-kateidenki Akihabara Head Office TO KANDA
TO UENO
SUBWAY GINZA LINE
CHUO-DORI ST.
Kakuta
Tsukumo Denki No.8 shop
Yamagiwa Duty Free
Hirose-musen Head Office
Shintoku Head Office
Nakaura No.3 shop
Onoden •
Laox Head Office
Manse Bashi
Horonix
Nishimura Denki No.2 shop
Shimura Plaza
Kanto Denshi Radio Dept.
Dinamic Audio
Ishimaru Denki No.3 shop
Ham Geppan
Chichibu Denki
Ishimaru Denki No.1 shop
Laox New-instrument Hall
Fukunaga Dengyo
Telephone Sound
Suzuran-do
Nishikawa Denshi Buhin
Ishimaru Maicon Center
Ishimaru Denki Head Office
• Video Center
CHUO & SOBU LINE
KANDA R.
TO KANDA
CHUO LINE
Livina Yamagiwa
Ishimaru Denki No.6 shop
Nikkyo Denki Shokai
TO KASUGA-DORI ST.
SHOHEIBASHI-DORI ST.
•Shohei bashi
←TO SUIDOBASHI
TO YOTSUYA-SHINJUKU

Yasukuni-dori and Hakusan-dori streets in the area around Jinbocho subway station are home to some 130 used book stores. Many of the books are on academic subjects, and many of the stores specialize in particular fields, such as Japanese literature, philosophy, art, or education. A number handle English and other foreign language books. The area is particularly lively during the weeklong Kanda Used Book Festival, held each year at the beginning of November. Bookworms aren't the only ones who will enjoy this neighborhood. From the Surugadai intersection to Ogawa-machi is Japan's largest collection of ski shops. They're open year-round, but naturally tend to be most crowded from early autumn through the end of the win-

ter. Among the best known and biggest stores are Victoria, Minami Sports.

Bookstore district: Kanda Jinbo-cho, Chiyoda-ku [S] Jinbocho Sta. ⊙ Hours vary; usually 10:00-18:30 [H] Vary, mostly Sun./Ski shop district: Kanda Ogawa-machi, Chiyoda-ku [S] Ogawamachi Sta. ⊙ Hours vary, usually 10:30-19:30 [H] Vary

KANDA BOOKSTORE DISTRICT

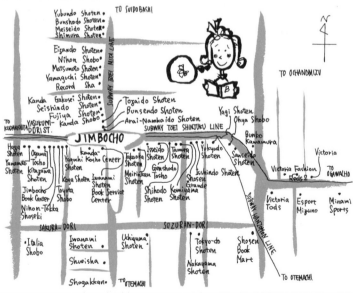

WASEDA BOOKSTORE DISTRICT
早稲田古書街

Walking from Takadanobaba Station along Waseda-dori toward Waseda University, from the Meiji-dori intersection you will come upon a number of used book stores along both sides of the street. The 40-odd shops each have their own specialties, mostly literature and the arts. Some also offer new books at discount prices. For a week in early October each year, the Waseda Blue Sky Used Book Mart takes place at the nearby Anahachiman Shrine. It's a good opportunity to find that rare book you've been looking for. This area is also well endowed with coffeehouses — ideal for a break after hunting for books. Recommendations include Chez Nous and Le Petit Nuit .

Nishi-Waseda, Shinjuku-ku [S] [JR] Takadanobaba Sta. [S] Waseda Sta. ⏰ Hours vary; usually 10:00-19:00 [H] Vary; usually Sun.

WASEDA BOOKSTORE DISTRICT

SHOPPING

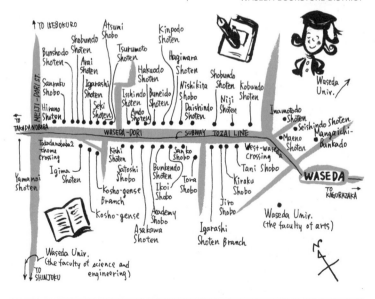

If Akihabara is Japan's mecca for discount electronic goods, Ameyoko serves the same function for daily necessities. Located along the railway tracks between JR Okachimachi and Ueno stations, it comprises over 500 stalls and shops. Foods, clothes, shoes, sports equipment, cosmetics, gems, precious metals, watches — name it and they probably have it. And all at considerable savings. Jeans for example begin at about ¥1,000, and top-brand handbags at up to 60% off retail price.

AMEYOKO MARKET

This area began in the years after World War II as a market for surplus U.S. Army supplies, and the legacy is still visible in the army jackets, bomber jackets, and other military gear for sale here. Altogether cleaner and more orderly is Ameyoko Center Building, a new, triangular building containing a number of retailers.

Ueno, Taito-ku [S] [JR] Ueno Sta. Okachimachi Sta. ⊙ Hours vary; usually 10:00-19:00 [H] Vary; usually 3rd Wed.

Located just behind the glitter of Ginza is the very different world of Tsukiji. This is Tokyo's wholesale food market, particularly for fish, but also for vegetables, fruits, and processed foods. The market is divided into separate areas, one for professional dealers and retailers, one for ordinary consumers. It's a popular sightseeing destination: the long rows of huge frozen tuna are an unforgettable sight. But you can also buy, and the savings are considerable, since everything is at wholesale prices. For the best deal, buy large quantities (i.e., in kilogram units), and plan on keeping a stock of frozen fish in your freezer. It's a big area, and by the time you've made the rounds you're likely to be both tired and hungry. One obvious choice is *sushi*, fresh from the market. Try Sushisei, Kibunzushi, or Edogin. Another popular meal here is *ramen* noodles, especially at Inoue, on Shin-ohashi-dori.

Tsukiji, Chuo-ku [S] Tsukiji Sta. ⊙ Hours vary; usually 6:00-12:00 [H] Sun., hol.

TSUKIJI (TOKYO WHOLESALE MARKET)

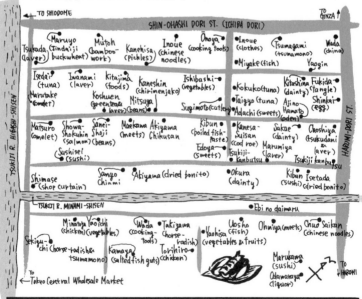

KAPPABASHI KITCHEN SUPPLY DISTRICT | 32
合羽橋道具街 | B1

KAPPABASHI KITCHEN SUPPLY DISTRICT

Just as professional cooks go to Tsukiji to buy their ingredients, they come to Kappabashi to buy their tools. Though less than a kilometer long, there are some 200 restaurant supply shops in this area, which is located between Kototoi-dori and Asakusa-dori midway between Ueno and Asakusa. They sell not only pots and pans, but every related item from chef's hats and *noren* curtains to tables and chairs. One favorite souvenir is the wax models of food made for restaurants to display in their windows (wax *sushi* from ¥350 a piece). Prices are uniformly low. While about 90% of the clients here are in the food service trade, almost all the stores will sell to ordinary shoppers.

Nishi-Asakusa & Matsugaya, Taito-ku S Tawara-cho Sta. ⊙ Hours vary; usually 9:00-17:30 H Vary; usually Sun., hol.

SHOPPING

ASAKUSABASHI TOY STORE DISTRICT | –
浅草橋玩具問屋街 | –

The myriad shops selling dolls, toys, games, stationery, and miscellaneous goods along Edo-dori near JR Asakusabashi Station together make up Japan's main wholesale district for these items. While these shops exist to sell to retailers, they don't mind the rest of us. Prices begin at 20-30% below standard retail prices and can be lowered even further by bargaining. That makes Asakusabashi an excellent place to stock up on large quantities of supplies for parties and other events. It's also interesting just to window shop: the variety of items is extraordinary, and you're certain to find all kinds of strange little toys and

ASAKUSABASHI TOY STORE DISTRICT

knickknacks.

Asakusabashi & Yanagibashi, Taito-ku S JR Asakusabashi Sta. ⊙ Hours vary; usually 10:00-18:00 H Vary; usually Sun. & hol.

LAFORET HARAJUKU

	22
ラフォーレ原宿	C5

Harajuku's famed fashion building brings together a complete collection of designer brands. It's also a popular local meeting place. The two yearly sales, in January and July, offer bargains throughout the entire building. Altogether, an unmissable Harajuku sight.

1-11-6 Jingu-mae, Shibuya-ku ☎ 3475-0411 ⒿⓇ Harajuku Sta. Ⓢ Meiji-jingu-mae Sta. 🕙 11:00-20:00 Ⓗ None Ⓒ JCB, DN, VISA, MC, AMEX, others

LAFORET HARAJUKU

HARAJUKU QUEST

	22
原宿クエスト	B5

Still gleaming and new, this beautiful building combines fashion boutiques and restaurants into an adult shopping/dining center. It's also pleasant just to stroll and look around, which has helped make Quest the newest place of choice for meeting friends when in the Harajuku area.

1-13-14 Jingu-mae, Shibuya-ku ☎ 3470-6331 ⒿⓇ Harajuku Sta. Ⓢ Meiji-jingu-mae Sta. 🕙 11:00-20:00 (Restaurants -23:00) Ⓗ None Ⓒ JCB, VISA, MC, AMEX, others.

VIVRE 21

	22
ビブレ 21	D5

You'll spot this building by the cafe at the entrance. Cafe Vieben, with its sidewalk patio, attracts a clearly international clientele. Inside are a variety of adult fashion boutiques, including names like Kikuchi Takeo and Trussardi. Bon Menage, in the basement, sells fine Western and Japanese dining and kitchen ware.

5-10-1 Jingu-mae, Shibuya-ku ☎ 3498-2221 ⒿⓇ Harajuku Sta. Ⓢ Meiji-jingu-mae Sta., Omote-sando Sta. 🕙 11:00-20:00 Ⓗ None Ⓒ JCB, DN, VISA, MC, AMEX, others.

VIVRE 21

BELL COMMONS

	23
ベルコモンズ	F3

This Aoyama landmark is filled with shops offering upscale, adult-oriented goods and services. About a third of the stores specialize in fashionable clothing . Another third are restaurants and cafes, with the remainder selling miscellaneous fashion items. The quality of all is uniformly high. Prominently located on Aoyama-dori.

2-14-6 Kita-Aoyama, Minato-ku ☎ 3475-8121 Ⓢ Gaien-mae Sta. 🕙 11:00-20:00 Ⓗ None Ⓒ JCB, DN, VISA, MC, AMEX, others

SEIBU DEPARTMENT STORE (Shibuya Branch) — 25

西武デパート — E3

Known for its distinctive advertisements and progressive image, Seibu is among Japan's leading department stores. Here in youthful Shibuya, it encompasses a number of separate buildings: A-Kan (building), entirely devoted to women's fashions; B-Kan, similarly for men's fashions; Seed-Kan, featuring imported clothing; Loft-Kan, for party supplies, tableware, stationery, and other day-to-day essentials; and Wave, located within Loft-Kan, offering a wide range of CDs, records, and other recorded audio and video. Both Seed-Kan and Loft-Kan have bars open until 2 am.

21-1 Udagawa-cho, Shibuya-ku ☎ 3462-0111 ⒮ ⒭Ⓡ Shibuya Sta. ⏱ 10:00-19:00 Ⓗ Wed. Ⓒ JCB, DN, VISA, MC, AMEX, others

109

109 — 24

109 — Ichi-Maru-Kyu — C4

Perhaps Shibuya's best known fashion building, 109 (☎ 3477- 5111) is the unmistakable round tower overlooking the entire station area. It has three sister shops nearby: 109-2 (☎ 3477-8111), mostly for teens; One-oh-Nine (☎ 3477-6711), for a slightly older clientele than 109; and One-oh-Nine 30's (☎ 3477-8311), aimed at shoppers in their 30s. Wander around all four and you're bound to find something you like.

⒮ ⒭Ⓡ Shibuya Sta. ⏱ 10:00-21:00 (shops) 11:00-22:30 (restaurants) Ⓗ None Ⓒ JCB, DN, VISA, MC, AMEX, others.

FROM 1ST — 23

フロム ファースト — H5

Even by the high standards of the Harajuku area, this collection of women's boutiques has gained a reputation for taste and sophistication. Issey Miyake and Moga are among the shops represented. There are also several restaurants and a bar that's open until 2 am.

5-3-10 Minami-Aoyama, Minato-ku ☎ 3499-3479 ⒮ Omote-sando Sta. ⏱ 11:00-20:00(shop hours vary) Ⓗ None Ⓒ JCB, DN, VISA, MC, AMEX, others.

SHOPPING

Ark Hills—City within a City

Walking from Roppongi toward Tameike will bring you to a group of huge, impressive new buildings. This is Ark Hills, a sub-city fully equipped with its own business, communications, entertainment, and housing complexes. The name is an acronym for "Akasaka-Roppongi Knot", Akasaka and Roppongi being the two parts of town on either side. Among these buildings are to be found the offices of Bank of America and other foreign banks; TV Asahi's broadcasting center, ANA Hotel, and Suntory Hall. One novelty of interest on the top floor of the main building is the bath and toilet showroom of a company called INAX. There are also a number of cafes and restaurants. Exploring it all could take half a day. ⒮ Roppongi Sta.

WAVE (Roppongi Branch)

	16
ウェイヴ	A6

The unusual exterior has become a Roppongi landmark. Inside, all is devoted to music and other recordings: tapes, records, CDs, videos, and so on, mostly imported. They even have a recording studio on the premises. The movie theater in the basement screens a number of European films.

6-2-27 Roppongi, Minato-ku ☎ 3408-0111 [S] Roppongi Sta. ◷ 11:00-22:00 [H] 1st & 3rd Wed. [C] JCB, DN, VISA, MC, AMEX, others.

WAVE

AXIS

	16
アクシス	D6

Chic and stylish, the white exterior of this Roppongi building makes its easily located and a good rendezvous spot. Inside are a number of equally fashionable shops, beginning with the Living Motif interior goods store on the ground floor. Newest of the stores is Biblio Phile, selling English and other Western books on the second floor. The whole building is yet another of the many places in Tokyo that are perfectly enjoyable just for window-shopping.

5-17-1 Roppongi, Minato-ku ☎ 3587-2781 [S] Roppongi Sta. ◷11:00-19:00(Shops hours vary) [H] Sun or Mon. [C] JCB, DN, VISA, MC, AMEX. others

TOKYU HANDS (Shibuya Branch)

	24
東急ハンズ	C3

Whatever your hobby or handicraft, you'll find all the materials and tools you need at this immensely popular do-it-yourself department store. The first floor features outdoor-related goods, games, and party supplies. On the 2F level are travel items and bath and grooming supplies. Interior goods, including knock-down furniture, are found on 3F. On the next floor up are leather craft supplies, models, and fabrics. Stationery supplies, including a selection of unique ballpoint pens, occupy the 5F level; electrical goods on 6F; and a bookshop on 7F. The latter has a good selection of English-language books. In the basement are lumber and carpentry tools and supplies. Helpful sales staff on all floors can offer advice and assistance to make sure you get exactly what you need. There are so many novel, beautifully designed items here that you could probably spend a whole day just browsing.

12-18 Udagawa-cho, Shibuya-ku ☎ 5489-5111 [S] [JR] Shibuya Sta. ◷ 10:00-20:00 [H] 2nd & 3rd Wed. [C] JCB, DN, VISA, MC, AMEX, others

AXIS

LAZY SUSAN 23

レイジー・スーザン	F4

The place to come if you're planning a party. Aside from party goods, they stock bags, watches, and their own line of tableware. There's a sophisticated New Yorkish style to everything they sell. A favorite with foreigners in Japan.

3-8-38 -1F Minami-Aoyama, Minato-ku ☎ 3403 -9546 S Omote-sando Sta. ⏰ 11:00-20:00 H None C JCB, DN, VISA, MC, AMEX, others.

LAZY SUSAN

ZONART 24

ゾナルト	A2

Specializing in wrapping paper and related supplies, this shop is a long-time favorite with its largely female clientele. The brightly lit interior features beautiful displays of more than 200 kinds of wrapping paper and 400 types of ribbons, as well as various boxes, bags, cards, etc. If your wrapping skills aren't up to par, bring your package here, choose your wrapping materials and (for a moderate fee) they'll do it for you.

9-5 Kamiyama-cho, Shibuya-ku ☎ 3467-4471 S JR Shibuya Sta. ⏰ 11:00-19:00 H Sun. C DC

FLAX 22

フラックス	C6

Sells stationery goods, mostly imported. System notebooks and looseleaf binders are among the many well designed items in stock. Recommended are the wristwatches (¥10,000), a recent favorite among customers here. Well worth a stop on any walk around the Harajuku area.

Miyazaki Bldg. 1F 6-28-5 Jingumae, Shibuya-ku ☎ 3407-3590 S Meiji-jingu-mae Sta. ⏰ 11:00-19:30 H None C JCB, DN, VISA, MC, AMEX, others

FLAX

PAPER WEIGHT 25

ペーパー・ウェイト	G6

Miscellaneous interior decor items in a shop resembling an art gallery. All are designed and manufactured for this store, with emphasis on novelty and sophistication. The current bestseller: a combination kaleidoscope/music box for ¥6,800. A good place for finding the perfect gift.

1-35-16 Ebisu-Nishi, Shibuya-ku ☎ 3464-1686 P Tokyu-Toyoko Line Daikan-yama Sta. ⏰ 11:30-19:30 H None C JCB, DN, VISA, MC, AMEX, others

···ON SUNDAYS | 23

オン・サンデーズ | E3

Art and photography books in a chic setting. They also feature a large selection of stationery items. The emphasis is on lesser known, quality products from around the world. Of particular note are the postcards — more than 4,000 varieties.

3-7-6 Jingu-mae, Shibuya-ku ☎ 3470-1424 [S] Gaien-mae Sta. 🕐 11:00-20:00 [H] Mon. [C] VISA, AMEX

TOWER RECORDS | 24

タワーレコード | C3

Tokyo's own branch of the well known U.S. retail record chain. That means the latest selection of imported pop music, jazz, etc., all at low prices. It's a good place to find imported versions of records that are out of print in Japan, which helps explain the constant crowds here. Whatever you're looking for, odds are they'll have it.

Village 80 Bldg. 2,3F 39-2 Udagawa-cho, Shibuya-ku ☎ 3496-3661 [S] [JR] Shibuya Sta. 🕐 10:00-22:00 [H] None [C] None

GINZA KUROSAWA | 12

銀座クロサワ | C3

This fashionable brick building, located on the Ginza's main avenue, houses a complete range of stationery and office supplies. Noteworthy are the greeting cards near the entrance, the wrapping paper and ribbons in the basement, and the stationery sets on the M2F level. Many are imported directly by the store, and the selection shows a fine sense of style.

6-9-2 Ginza, Chuo-ku ☎ 3571-8441 [S] Ginza Sta. 🕐 10:30-20:00 (Sun. & hol. -19:00) [H] None [C] JCB, DN, VISA, MC, AMEX, others

TOWER RECORDS

ITO-YA | 12

伊東屋 | D4

ITO-YA

This is easily Tokyo's favorite stationery store. The nine floors are filled with hobby items, art supplies, stationery, and office supplies. The greeting cards on the ground floor are extremely popular and make fine gifts to take home. Also good for gifts and a favorite with foreign customers are the *washi* (traditional Japanese paper) items in the 7F art supply area. After shopping, drop by the gallery and tea lounge on the ninth floor.

2-7-15 Ginza, Chuo-ku ☎ 3561-8311 [S] Ginza Sta. 🕐 09:30-19:00 (Sun.& hol. 10:00-18:00) [H] None [C] JCB, DN, VISA, MC, AMEX, others

KINOKUNIYA BOOK STORE

KINOKUNIYA BOOK STORE | 27

紀伊國屋書店 | Kinokuniya Shoten | **E3**

If you're looking for books in Shinjuku, you need look no further. Kinokuniya offers a wide assortment of western books and magazines, and can order from abroad anything they don't have. You can even subscribe to foreign magazines here. The hall on the 4th floor presents performances by popular young drama groups.

3-17-7 Shinjuku, Shinjuku-ku ☎ 3354-0131 S JR Shinjuku Sta. ◎ 10:00-19:00 H 3rd Wed. C JCB, DN, VISA, MC, AMEX, others.

SHIMADA FOREIGN BOOK STORE | 23

嶋田洋書 | Shimada Yosho | **F6**

The 7,000-8,000 foreign titles here make for an enjoyable browse. About one-third are related to automobiles, with the remainder on subjects like design, crafts, and interior decoration. The emphasis is on photos, pictures, and graphics, with no literature, history or the like. Many of the customers are specialists in the fields represented here.

5-9-19 Minami-Aoyama, Minato-ku ☎ 3407-3863 S Omote-sando Sta. ◎ 11:00-20:00 (Sun. & hol. -19:00) H None C JCB, DN, VISA, MC, AMEX

JENA FOREIGN BOOK STORE | 12

イエナ洋書店 | Iena Yoshoten | **C3**

Located in the midst of busy Ginza, this store handles a complete selection of imported books (other than specialist books). The 50,000 or so titles on hand at any one time range from pictorial books on film, music, and photography to paperback potboilers. The illustrated art books make this a favorite bookstore even among Japanese.

5-6-1 Ginza, Chuo-ku ☎ 3571-2980 S Ginza Sta. ◎ 10:30-19:50 (Sun. 12:00-18:30) H hol. C JCB, DN, VISA, MC, AMEX, others.

MARUZEN (Nihonbashi Branch) | 18

丸善 | | **C4**

A bookstore with a history of more than 100 years. Of the some 300,000 books in stock at the Nihonbashi shop, about half are in English and other foreign languages. The pictorial book section receives especially high marks, with more than 12,000 titles, mostly from Europe and the U.S. It's enjoyable just to browse through them and see the differences in style and color usage in books from various countries. The staff is helpful and knowledgeable.

2-3-10 Nihonbashi, Chuo-ku ☎ 3272-7211 S Nihonbashi Sta. ◎ 10:00-18:30 H Sun. C JCB, DN, VISA, MC, AMEX, others.

MARUZEN

KIDDY LAND

	22
キディランド	D6

From basement to fifth floor, this building is crammed with toys of every imaginable type: dolls, stuffed animals, games, models (some radio-controlled), party supplies and much more. It's also perpetually crowded with young people, even by the standards of Harajuku. Enough of the staff speak English that language shouldn't be a problem.

6-1-9 Jingu-mae, Shibuya-ku ☎ 3409-3431 JR Harajuku Sta. Ⓢ Omote-sando Sta. ◷ 10:00-20:00 H 3rd Tue. C JCB, DN, VISA, MC, AMEX, others

ANOTHER ONE

	–
アナザワン	–

Bring in a photograph of someone and this shop will create a doll that looks just like him or her. It can be anybody — your husband or wife, your new baby, your neighbor. Be prepared however to spend about ¥20,000. Ordering requires a certain amount of discussion, so if your Japanese isn't up to it, bring a Japanese friend along.

2-14-7 Jiyugaoka, Meguro-ku ☎ 3717-2230 P Tokyu-Toyoko Line Jiyugaoka Sta. ◷ 11:00-19:00 H Wed. C JCB, DN, VISA, MC, AMEX

BIRIKEN SHOKAI

	23
ビリケン商会	H6

Take a trip back to nostalgia at this shop specializing in Made-in-Japan stamped metal toys and cartoon character dolls from the 1950s and 60s. It's a small store, but filled with now-rare toys. Don't miss Ultraman, Japan's greatest super hero.

5-17-6 Minami-Aoyama, Minato-ku ☎ 3400-2214 Ⓢ Omote-sando Sta. ◷ 12:00-19:00 H Mon. & 2nd Tue. C None

HAKUHINKAN TOY PARK

	12
博品館トイパーク	B3

This modern toy shop in the Ginza claims to be Japan's largest. On the first floor are gift items, party supplies, and interior goods. The second floor features games, puzzles, and models. On the 3F level are various toys and games for infants and young children. Dolls are the specialty on the fourth floor. Whatever the item, the selection is wide. The fifth and higher floors house a theater and a number of restaurants. A favorite Ginza stop for travelers from abroad.

8-8-11 Ginza, Chuo-ku ☎ 3571-8008 Ⓢ JR Shinbashi Sta. ◷ 11:00-20:00 H None C JCB, DN, VISA, MC, AMEX, others

KIDDY LAND

CUDDLY BROWN

	25
カドゥリーブラウン	G6

You might guess it from the name: this shop sells teddy bears. They also have other species of stuffed creatures, as well as tableware, clothes, and even bear-shaped candies. Bestsellers include leather coin purses and golf balls decorated with pictures of bears. One peek into the window from the street and you'll probably want to come in and take a look.

4-5 Sarugaku-cho, Shibuya-ku ☎ 3477-7178 P Tokyu-Toyoko Line Daikanyama Sta. ◷ 11:00-19:00 (Sun. & hol. 10:30-18:30) H None C JCB, VISA, AMEX, others

KID BLUE MUSE | 22

キッドブルー・ムーサ | D3

This shop sells its own line of women's lingerie and nightwear in soft pastel colors. The stylish designs have earned it an enthusiastic clientele. Worth a look to see the colors and designs for yourself. Pajamas from ¥20,000.

Flora Harajuku Bldg. 1F 3-34-9 Jingu-mae, Shibuya-ku ☎ 3470-5885 Ⓢ Gaien-mae Sta. Ⓣ 11:00-20:00 Ⓗ None Ⓨ ★★ Ⓒ JCB, DN, VISA, MC, AMEX

F.O.B. CO-OP | 20

フォブ・コープ | C3

Chosen for quality of design and ease of use, the goods sold here are favorites with stylists who plan features for "living" sections of Japanese publications. In addition to tableware, you'll find stationery and clothing items, including imports from the U.S. and France. Prices are moderate. They offer a 10% discount on rainy days, so it's a fine place for a date when it's raining – and there's even a cafe.

5-10-32 Minami-Azabu, Minato-ku ☎ 3446-5332 Ⓢ Hiro-o Sta. Ⓣ 11:00-21:00 (Sun. & hol. 12: 00-20:00) Ⓗ None Ⓒ JCB, VISA

ORIENTAL BAZAAR | 22

オリエンタルバザー | D6

A major name in Japanese traditional artworks and antiques. Oriental Bazaar is especially popular among visitors to Japan seeking gifts to take home, offering plenty of ideas if you're having trouble finding the right presents. The vast assortment of Japanese-style goods makes it a fine place just for window-shopping.

5-9-13 Jingu-mae, Shibuya-ku ☎ 3400-3933 Ⓢ Omote-sando Sta. Ⓣ 09:30-18:30 Ⓗ Thur. Ⓒ JCB, DN, VISA, MC, AMEX, others

GRAIN DAILE | 24

グランデール | D1

This popular small shop, with its wooden floor and shelves, is crowded with stylish yet practical tableware. Whether from the store's own line or unusual imported designs, the products are durable and the prices are reasonable.

1-6-1 Jinnan, Shibuya-ku ☎ 3463-7519 Ⓢ Ⓙ Ⓡ Shibuya Sta. Ⓣ 10:30-19:30 Ⓗ None Ⓒ None

NOUVEAU | 16

ヌーボー | C5

A favorite among young women, Roppongi's Nouveau sells miscellaneous imported decorative and gift items. Currently popular are the cat ornaments (¥1,000-1,500) and clocks (from ¥5,000). An enjoyable browse.

Koyasu Bldg. 1F 7-14-7 Roppongi, Minato-ku ☎ 3402-7557 Ⓢ Roppongi Sta. Ⓣ 10:30-23:00 Ⓗ None Ⓒ None

ORIENTAL BAZAAR

YUZAWAYA — —
ユザワヤ

This big crafts shop comprises four separate buildings, and they also have branches in Urawa (Saitama Prefecture) and Tachikawa. Fabrics, sewing supplies, curtains, and *washi* traditional Japanese paper are just some of the items to be found here. Especially popular is the selection of yarns, many imported, in the No. 6 building. Discounts are offered on almost all items.

8-23-5 Nishi-Kamata, Ota-ku ☎ 3734-4141 [JR] Kamata Sta. ⏰ 10:00-19:00 [H] None [C] JCB, DN, VISA, AMEX

JANNU 30
ジャヌー A3

A sportswear shop selling its own line of clothing, mainly for tennis. Windbreakers for ¥8,000 to ¥16,000; stadium jackets for ¥28,000 to ¥32,000. They'll even make uniforms for your team (¥3,800-13,000). They also sell rackets and other sporting goods, and can order imported items for you.

3-16-14 Mejiro, Toshima-ku ☎ 3951-1775 [JR] Mejiro Sta. ⏰ 11:00- 21:00 (Sun. -19:00) [H] None [C] JCB, DN, VISA, MC, AMEX, others

AMERICAN PHARMACY 12
アメリカン・ファーマシィ D1

Like any hometown American drug store, this is more than a pharmacy: they also stock a wide range of stationery and sundries, mostly imported. Greeting cards include both American cartoon-style cards and the simple Japanese style. Near Hibiya Station and easily located, it's well worth a look.

Hibiya Park Bldg. 1F Yuraku-cho, Chiyoda-ku ☎ 3271-4034 [S] [JR] Yuraku-cho Sta. [S] Hibiya Sta. ⏰ 09:00-19:00 (Sun. & hol. 11:00-18:00) [H] Sun. [C] JCB, DN, VISA, MC, AMEX, others.

AGAIN 23
アゲイン F3

In an interior reminiscent of an up-country hotel somewhere in Kenya, this unusual boutique can supply everything you'll need for your next safari, from clothing to the smallest accessories. The biggest emphasis is on golf equipment, but everything here has an element of fun.

Aoyama Bell Commons Bldg. 2F Kita-Aoyama, Minato-ku☎3475-8030 [S] Gaien-mae Sta.⏰ 11:00-20:00 [H] None [C] JCB, DN, VISA, MC, AMEX

AMERICAN PHARMACY

TADA SPORTS 20
多田スポーツ C5

This discount outlet for sports shoes has found an enthusiastic young clientele. Adidas and other top brand-name athletic shoes go for 20% to 50% off list price, and the selection is vast. They're also among the first to offer models newly introduced in the U.S.

5-19-5 Hiro-o, Shibuya-ku ☎ 3473-1924 [S] Hiro-o Sta. ⏰ 11:00-20:00 [H] Mon. [C] None

KINOKUNIYA	23
紀ノ国屋	F6

A landmark on fashionable Aoyama-dori (Aoyama Street), this international supermarket stocks everything from oatmeal to caviar. The huge selection of imported foods make it a favorite among foreign residents. They offer their own fresh-baked breads and pastries. Cash registers are all on the second floor. Grocery shopping at its most comfortable.

3-11-7 Kita-Aoyama, Minato-ku ☎ 3409-1231 [S] Omote-sando Sta. ⊙ 09:30-20:00 [H] None [C] None

NATIONAL AZABU SUPERMARKET	20
ナショナル麻布スーパー	D5

Renowned for its large stock of foods of the world, with a particularly fine selection of wines and cheeses. And if you need reading material for your ride home after shopping, imported books and magazines are available as well. Conveniently close to Hiro-o Station.

4-5-2 Minami-Azabu, Minato-ku ☎ 3442-3181 [S] Hiro-o Sta. ⊙ 09:30-18:30 [H] None [C] None

NATURAL HOUSE (Aoyama Branch)	23
ナチュラルハウス	F5

Natural foods that are good for you — that's the basic concept at Natural House. It means foods like organic vegetables (i.e., grown without pesticides), pasta made from Japanese *konnyaku*, low-salt sauces, and low-calorie cakes and pastries. They even offer fragrance-free cosmetics.

3-6-18 Kita-Aoyama, Minato-ku ☎ 3498-2277 [S] Omote-sando Sta. ⊙ 10:00-22:00 [H] None [C] None

KINOKUNIYA

MEIDI-YA(Roppongi Branch)	16
明治屋	B5

The stylish brick exterior marks the Roppongi outlet of the well known Meidi-ya supermarket. A wonderful place for imported foods, as well as their own line of jams, soups, etc. The location draws a largely international clientele. Other branches can be found in Hiro-o and Ginza; the latter is especially good for wine and cheese. All have good stocks of sweets and candies — whether it's honey roasted cashews or gummy bears, you'll find them here.

7-15-14 Roppongi, Minato-ku ☎ 3401-8511 [S] Roppongi Sta. ⊙ 10:00-22:00 [H] None [C] JCB, DN, VISA, MC

NATURAL HOUSE

NISHIURA-HONPO | 19

西浦本舗 | F6

A Japanese pottery shop established in 1877. While many areas of Japan have developed their own styles of ceramics, this shop concentrates on the *Kiyomizuyaki* style of Kyoto. The stock ranges from practical pieces like tea cups and plates to exquisite (and expensive) flower vases and tea ceremony items. It's fascinating just to look at the various styles — and some of the smaller pieces make excellent gifts to take back home.

Nishiura Bldg. 2-2-1 Nihonbashi Ningyocho, Chuo-ku ☎ 3667-5851 [S] Ningyocho Sta. ◎ 9:00-18:00 [H] Sun.& hol. [C] JCB, DN, VISA, MC, AMEX, others

SUKEROKU

KONDO SHOTEN | –

近藤商店 | –

Specializing in traditional Japanese bamboo crafts. Many are for restaurant and other commercial use, so the quality is high and the prices reasonable. Items like *soba* noodle trays (¥4,000-5,000) and large baskets offer uses limited only by your imagination.

3-1-13 Matsugaya, Taito-ku ☎ 3841-3372 [S] Tawaracho Sta. ◎ 9:30 - 17:30 [H] Sun., hol. [C] None

KUROEYA | 18

黒江屋 | D4

Lacquerware is an important Japanese craft, and while not cheap, it represents a unique facet of this nation's culture. This famous shop offers pieces from Aizu, Wajima, and all other major lacquerware regions. Bowls from ¥2,000 to ¥10,000; round trays from ¥3,000 to ¥20,000.

1-2-6 Nihonbashi, Chuo-ku ☎ 3272-0948 [S] Nihonbashi Sta. ◎ 9:00-17:00 [H] Sun. & hol. 1st, 2nd & 3rd Sat. [C] JCB, DN, VISA, MC, AMEX, others

SARUYA | 19

さるや | F6

And toothpicks are the exclusive stock in trade at the 270-year-old Saruya. Every of their toothpicks is hand carved, and the store's many fans appreciate both their strength and their fresh woody fragrance.

18-10 Nihonbashi Koami-cho, Chuo-ku ☎ 3666-3906 [S] Ningyo-cho Sta. ◎ 9:00-17:00 [H] Sun. hol. & 3rd Sat. [C] None

SUKEROKU | 32

助六 | B3

One of the many Japanese craft shops lining *Nakamise*, the road leading to Asakusa's Senso-ji Temple. Sukeroku sells traditional toys, as it has since the late Edo period — the current proprietor is the fifth generation. Among the 3,500 items in stock are toys decorated with Asakusa festival motifs, *hina* (Girls' Festival) dolls, and papier-mâché dogs. A good selection from less than ¥1,000.

2-3-1 Asakusa, Taito-ku ☎ 3844-0577 [S] Asakusa Sta. ◎ 10:30-18:30 [H] Thur. [C] None

KASACHO | 29

傘長 | G5

Nothing is more evocative of old Japan than paper lanterns and waxed paper umbrellas, the specialty of this shop. The interior is in fact lined with lanterns, all made by the owner himself. While some are now rare and consequently fairly expensive, there is a selection of cheaper items, many of which can be used for interior accents and other decoration. Lanterns from about ¥2,500. .

2-4 Kanda Tacho, Chiyoda-ku ☎ 3256-7007 S JR Kanda Sta. 🕐 09:00-18:00 H Sun. & hol. C None

ISETATSU | 31

いせ辰 | A2

The specialty here is *Edo chiyogami*, a type of handmade paper long produced in Tokyo and still popular today, especially among women. Located in Yanaka, a neighborhood that still retains the *shitamachi* (downtown) atmosphere of old *Edo*, the shop greets you with a large papier-mâché dog at the entrance. Established in the Edo period, Isetatsu sells about 1,000 types of colorful *chiyogami* and small items made from it. Bestsellers include memo books (from ¥480), letter sets (from ¥550), and good luck charms.

2-18-9 Yanaka, Taito-ku ☎ 3823-1453 S Sendagi Sta. 🕐 10:00-18:00 H None C None

YOSHITOKU

BINGOYA | 27

備後屋 | H1

The various crafts from different parts of Japan and the way they reflect the customs of their respective regions is a constant source of interest. This shop offers a chance to see a complete range, from Aomori in the north to the islands of Okinawa in the south.

10-6 Wakamatsu-cho, Shinjuku-ku ☎ 3202-8778 S Waseda Sta. 🕐 10:00-19:00 H Mon. C JCB, DN, VISA, MC, AMEX, others

YOSHITOKU | 29

吉徳 | H3

Twice a year — in March and May — the Japanese traditionally decorate their homes with dolls. Wholesalers and retailers specializing in these dolls are clustered in the old downtown area of Asakusa-bashi. The oldest of them all, founded in 1711, is Yoshitoku. The tiny, charming dolls sold here, each with its own impeccable face.

1-9-14 Asakusa-bashi, Taito-ku ☎ 3863-4419 S JR Asakusa-bashi Sta. 🕐 9:30-17:30 H Sun. (open daily Jan. 5 - May 5) C JCB, DN, VISA, MC, AMEX, others

HAIBARA | 18

はいばら | D5

A *washi* (traditional Japanese paper) shop established in 1806 and has the highest reputation: the novelist Yasunari Kawabata had his personal stationery made here. In stock are various papers from throughout Japan, mostly at moderate prices. Examples include stationery decorated with Japanese-style drawings (¥560 for ten sheets), and *chiyogami* (Japanese paper printed with colord figures, ¥120-300 per sheet).

2-7-6 Nihonbashi, Chuo-ku ☎ 3272-3801 S Nihonbashi Sta. 🕐 9:30-17:30 (Sat. -17:00) H Sun. & hol. C VISA

SHOPPING

ECHIGOYA | 12

越後屋 | **D4**

A long-established *kimono* shop on Ginza's main street. A wide variety of *kimonos* are on display, all of proper classical design — Echigoya, after all, is over 200 years old — and at correspondingly high prices. More affordable are the *obi* sashes of the shop's own design, from ¥60,000.

2-6-5 Ginza, Chuo-ku ☎ 3561-1583 Ⓢ Ginza Sta. Ⓞ 10:00-19:00 (Sun. & hol. 12:00-18:00) Ⓗ None Ⓒ JCB, DN, VISA, MC, AMEX, others

KISHIYA | 12

銀座きしや | **C3**

Located at the intersection of Ginza's Namiki and Miyuki- dori streets. All the *kimonos* in this kimono shop are selected under the discerning eye of the owner. 60% of them are based on original designes. "Traditional beauty for today" is the shop's motto, and it strives to offer contemporary *kimonos* that capture a sense of the past.

5-4-9 Ginza, Chuo-ku ☎ 3572-5291 Ⓢ Ginza Sta. Ⓞ 10:00-19:00 Ⓗ 2nd & 3rd Sun. Ⓒ JCB, DN, VISA, MC, AMEX, others

GINZA-KUNOYA | 12

銀座くのや | **C3**

The Ginza area is home to many *kimono* shops, but Ginza-Kunoya (established 1837) is somewhat unique: rather than *kimonos* themselves, they specialize in the various accessories that go with them. That includes, among other things, a complete line of their own *obi* sashes. Also of note is the selection of *furoshiki* wrapping cloths, from about ¥15,000.

6-9-8 Ginza, Chuo-ku ☎ 3571-2546 Ⓢ Ginza Sta. Ⓞ 11:00-20:00 Ⓗ None Ⓒ JCB, DN, VISA, MC, AMEX, others

AYAHATA | 17

あやはた | **E4**

While *kimonos* are undoubtedly lovely, their usual prices are simply out of reach for many people. This store offers a solution: used *kimonos*. *Obi* sashes, for example, are available here for as little as ¥3,000. Used *kimonos* make fine dressing gowns, while an *obi* can be used as a wall hanging or even as a tablecloth.

2-21-2 Akasaka, Minato-ku ☎ 3582-9969 Ⓢ Akasaka Sta. Ⓞ 11:00-20:00 Ⓗ Sun. & hol. Ⓒ JCB, DN, VISA, MC, AMEX, others

HOSENDO-KYUAMI | 32

宝扇堂久阿弥 | **B3**

Folding Japanese fans are an essential accessory to any *kimono*, and fans are the specialty of Asakusa's Hosendo-Kyuami. Especially highly regarded are the shop's *mai-ogi*, fans used in classical dance performances. They have over 600 different designs, as well as clothing and other accessories for Japanese dance.

1-19-6 Asakusa, Taito-ku ☎ 3845-5021 Ⓢ Asakusa Sta. Ⓞ 10:30-20:00 Ⓗ None Ⓒ JCB, DN, VISA, MC, AMEX, others

HOSENDO-KYUAMI

JUSANYA-KUSHITEN | 31
十三やくし店 | C5

Established in 1736, this shop is devoted to traditional Japanese combs. All their combs are made of boxwood, which is considered to be the finest wood for this purpose. Unfortunately it is now quite a rare wood, and prices are consequently high: ¥3,000 to ¥10,000 per comb. Splurge, however, and you'll have a valuable keepsake.

2-12-21 Ueno, Taito-ku ☎ 3831-3238 S JR Ueno Sta. 🕐 10:00-18:00 H 1st & 3rd Sun. C None

YONOYA | 32
よのや | B3

Yet another shop dating back to the Edo period, Asakusa's Yonoya also specializes in boxwood combs. You'll recognize it by the comb on the sign out front. Standard models from ¥3,000; deluxe versions for about ten times as much. Ornamental hairpins, also made from lacquered boxwood, from ¥4,800.

1-37-10 Asakusa, Taito-ku ☎ 3844-1755 S Asakusa Sta. 🕐 10:00-19:00 H Wed. C AMEX

FUJIYA | 32
ふじ屋 | B3

The *tenugui* Japanese-style towel is a most useful item. It serves as washcloth and towel and even as a kind of bathing cap. Or frame one for a touch of authentic Japanese artistry. Part of the traditional enjoyment is the large variety of designs available. Fujiya's *tenugui* are designed by the owner himself. Some feature Edo-era crests; others, nature poems from old Asakusa. Prices: ¥800-3,000.

2-2-15 Asakusa, Taito-ku ☎ 3841-2283 S Asakusa Sta. 🕐 10:00-19:00 H Thur. C None

ADACHIYA | 32
あだちや | C3

Asakusa's *Sanja Matsuri*, held every June, is one of Japan's three biggest and most famed festivals. Many of the revelers buy their *happi* coats and other costumes at this Asakusa shop. Realizing that costumes help set the mood for the entire event, Adachiya has a full stock of well-designed festival clothing, many designed by the shop itself. Quite a few of the colorful designs feature a distinctively contemporary look. Short *hanten* coats from about ¥2,600 to ¥16,000.

2-22-12 Asakusa, Taito-ku ☎ 3841-4915 S Asakusa Sta. 🕐 10:00-20:30 H Tue. C None

YONOYA

UBUKEYA | 19
うぶけや | F6

Ubuke means soft, downy hair. But what does that have to do with a knife shop? The answer is that an Ubukeya knife is so sharp that it cuts cleanly through even the softest hair. The people here have been handcrafting top-quality cutlery since 1783. Small scissors from ¥2,000; Japanese-style kitchen knives from ¥8,000.

3-9-2 Nihonbashi Ningyo-cho, Chuo-ku ☎ 3661-4851 S Ningyocho Sta. 🕐 09:00-19:00 (Sat. -18:00) H Sun. & hol. C None

The word "antique" covers a lot of ground, from artistic treasures to antique furniture to almost worthless old odds and ends. Most of the shops along Minami Aoyama Antique Street handle the higher end of this range: paintings, ceramics, books and other antiques of artistic value from Japan, China, and Korea. Running between Aoyama-dori and Metropolitan No. 3 Expressway, Antique Street is marked by no signs. Find it by going to Kinokuniya Supermarket — Antique Street starts at the gas station just across the street. The street is lined

MINAMI AOYAMA ANTIQUE STREET

with fashion boutiques, but interspersed among them (sometimes deep within the buildings) are more than 30 antique shops. Of particular note are the ten or so dealers on the 1st and 2nd floors of the Jintsu Building, located just after Hunting World on the right side of street coming from Aoyama- dori. "Karakusa" (☎ 3499-5858), specializing in now-popular *Imari* porcelain, and "Ikeda" (☎ 3407-5221), with its fine collection of ancient artifacts, are among the friendly shops here, and are well worth even a casual look.

S Omote-Sando Sta. ⏰ H Varies with stores

ROPPONGI ANTIQUE FAIR | 16

六本木アンティークフェア | D6

This event began in the late 1970s, about the time that many people in Japan were becoming interested in antiques. It's held in front of the Roi Building amid the discos and boutiques of Roppongi. The 20 or so vendors offer antiques of all sorts, with some specializing in particular fields: *Imari* pottery ("Mizuno"), ceramics ("Ben"), accessories; Japanese-style furniture, and antique tableware.

5-5-1 Roppongi, Minato-ku ☎ 3583-2081 Ⓢ Roppongi sta. Ⓒ 4th Thurs. & Fri. of each month, 8:00-20:00

NOGI SHRINE FLEA MARKET | 16

乃木神社古民具骨董市 | C3

Held regularly since 1976, this flea market attracts many foreign antique collectors. Some 30 vendors line both sides of the stone stairs into the shrine, selling mostly items that might have found in any ordinary Japanese home up until about 30 years ago — Taisho-era *tansu* (chests of drawers), low tea tables, cut glassware, old wall clocks, and used *kimonos*. Prices are often cheaper MARKETS than at antique shops.

Ⓢ Nogizaka Sta. Ⓒ 2nd Sun. of the month, sunrise to sunset

SHINJUKU HANAZONO SHRINE FLEA MARKET | 27

新宿花園神社骨董市 | F2

Hanazono Shrine is nestled among a stand of tall trees behind the Kabukicho area of Shinjuku. The flea market held here twice monthly offers a wide variety of items from old homes in the Japanese countryside, including *kimonos*, tableware, *hibachi* grills, and clocks. It's worth negotiating a while to get the best prices.

Ⓢ Shinjuku-sanchome Sta. Ⓒ 2nd & 3rd Sun. of the month, sunrise to sunset

SETAGAYA BOROICHI MARKET | —

世田谷ぼろ市 | —

Boroichi literally means "rag market", and indeed cloth and clothing were the specialties of this market when it was first held more than 400 years ago. It now takes place twice a year — on the 15th and 16th of each December and January — with a full kilometer of the road lined with 600-700 stalls. These days the items for sale include not only old clothing, but also antiques, tableware, potted plants, and foods. It's Tokyo's largest flea market, and the crowds begin arriving at sunrise. Be warned however: even half a day isn't enough to see it all.

Ⓟ Tokyu-Setagaya Line Kamimachi Sta.

Getting Around Cheaply

There's a lot to see in Tokyo, but you probably don't want to spend too much of your budget just getting from place to place. Walking is of course the cheapest way to get around, but it's a big city to cover on just your own two feet. A bicycle could help, but the amount of traffic on Tokyo's streets makes it difficult to recommend. The clear solution: public transport. Fortunately there's an inexpensive way to use Tokyo's public transport system as much as you like. Both the Toei and Eidan subways and the JR trains offer one-day passes good for unlimited use. Below are the details.

"Free Ticket" Passes (valid for one day only) 1. Eidan Subway Pass (for Eidan subway lines only) ...¥620 2. Toei Subway Pass (for Toei subway lines, buses, and streetcars) ...¥650 3. JR Tokyo Area Pass (for major JR train routes within the Tokyo area) ...¥720   4. Tokyo Area/Toei Pass (combines 2 and 3) ...¥1,100 5. Tokyo Pass (combines 1, 2 and 3)...¥1,400 Note: (1) is sold at Eidan subway stations; (2) at Toei subway stations and on board buses and streetcars;   (3) at JR stations both within and outside the Tokyo area; (4) at   Toei and JR stations;   (5) at Eidan, Toei, and JR stations.

ACCOMMODATION AND HEALTH

Keeping up with Tokyo means keeping up your energy....
A guide to rest, relaxation and fitness.

Tokyo Hotels

Hotels in Japan are not classified into official rankings as is done in Europe. This means you must rely on guidebooks and other knowledgeable sources for information about prices, facilities, and services. At virtually any hotel in Japan, however, you can be assured of clean, comfortable accommodations.

Hotels in Tokyo can be divided into two basic types: city hotels and business hotels. City hotels, like the Imperial Hotel and the Hotel Okura, meet high standards in every aspect of their facilities, services, and environment. Their rates are correspondingly high, with single rooms generally starting at about ¥10,000 per night. Business hotels, as their name suggests, cater primarily to people travelling on business, with emphasis on convenient locations and other functional accommodations. Single-room rates begin at around ¥5,000.

Try a Japanese Inn

In addition to Western-style hotels, Japan has its own traditional form of accommodation —— the *ryokan*, or Japanese inn. Staying at one of these establishments is an ideal way to experience Japanese life and customs. You'll stay in a *tatami*-floored room, eat Japanese food, and bathe in a large hot bath, often constructed of rocks and wood. And at night you'll sleep on a *futon*, Japanese-style bedding. Note that in our listings here, while we provide only addresses and telephone numbers for Western-style hotels, we offer additional information on each *ryokan* listed.

Relaxing at the Sento

One of the easiest ways to come face to face with the "real" Japan is at your local *sento*, or public bathhouse. The Japanese language has an expression literally meaning "naked encounter" , suggesting the basic sense of community that comes about when people bathe together. That is what makes the *sento* not just a place to soak and relax, but also an important social center. Bathhouses can be found in most any residential neighborhood, and open around 3 or 4 pm. daily. Entrance is a standard ¥310.

City Hotels

Imperial Hotel 帝国ホテル	1-1-1 Uchisaiwai-cho, Chiyoda-ku	☎3504-1111	BT32,000〜	**12・C1**
Palace Hotel パレスホテル	1-1-1 Marunouchi, Chiyoda-ku	☎3211-5211	BS19,000〜 BT25,500	**13・G1**
Ginza Tokyu Hotel 銀座東急ホテル	5-15-9 Ginza, Chuo-ku	☎3541-2411	BS15,800〜 BT25,800〜	**12・B3**
Akasaka Prince Hotel 赤坂プリンスホテル	1-2 Kioi-cho, Chiyoda-ku	☎3234-1111	BS22,000〜 BT30,000〜	**17・G1**
Tokyo Prince Hotel 東京プリンスホテル	3-3-1 Shiba-koen, Minato-ku	☎3432-1111	BS22,000〜 BT23,000〜	**15・E1**
Hotel Okura ホテルオークラ	2-10-4 Toranomon, Minato-ku	☎3582-0111	BS27,500〜 BT32,000〜	**17・G5**
Hotel New Otani ホテルニューオータニ	4-1 Kioi-cho, Chiyoda-ku	☎3265-1111	BS23,500〜 BT29,500〜	**17・F1**
ANA Hotel Tokyo 東京全日空ホテル	1-12-33 Akasaka, Minato-ku	☎3505-1111	BS21,000〜 BT29,000〜	**17・F4**
Hotel Century Hyatt ホテルセンチュリー・ハイアット	2-7-2 Nishi-Shinjuku, Shinjuku-ku	☎3349-0111	BS18,000〜 BT26,000〜	**26・A2**
Keio Plaza Hotel 京王プラザホテル	2-2-1 Nishi-Shinjuku, Shinjuku-ku	☎3344-0111	BS19,500〜 BT24,000〜	**26・B3**

＊S: single room BS: single room with bath T: twin room BT: twin room with bath
＊Rates do not include service charges and tax.

Business Hotels

Tokyo YMCA Hotel 東京YMCAホテル	7 Kanda-mitoshirocho, Chiyoda-ku	☎3293-1911	BS10,300〜	**29・F5**
Grand Central Hotel グランドセントラルホテル	2-2 Kanda-Tsukasa-cho, Chiyoda-ku	☎3256-3211	BS8,240〜	**29・G5**
Ginza Capital Hotel 銀座キャピタルホテル	2-1-4 Tsukiji, Chuo-ku	☎3543-8211	BS7,000〜	**13・D6**
Tokyo City Hotel 東京シティーホテル	1-9 Nihonbashi-Honcho, Chuo-ku	☎3270-7671	BS7,004〜	**19・G5**
Atagoyama Tokyu Inn 愛后山東急イン	1-6-6 Atago, Minato-ku	☎3431-0109	BS9,682〜	**17・H6**
Marroad Inn Akasaka マロウドイン赤坂	6-15-17 Akasaka, Minato-ku	☎3585-7611	BS8,000〜	**16・D3**

＊Rates include service charges and tax.

GAJOEN KANKO HOTEL	25
雅叙園観光ホテル	H6

This quintessential *ryokan* (Japanese inn) has been called "the ultimate expression of fine old Japanese architecture." It was originally built as a manor for a wealthy industrialist, employing the top architects, artists and craftsmen of the day. The entrance is on the second floor, while almost all of the first floor is occupied by dining and reception rooms. The paintings along the corridors between these rooms represent a rare and superb collection of *ukiyoe* and other masterpieces of the early Showa period. In contrast to the traditional Japanese exterior, the main bath is of modern design and color scheme, and large enough to accommodate 40 bathers at a time. The atmosphere of this unique inn is further enhanced by its location on the Meguro River.

1-8-1 Shimo-Meguro, Meguro-ku ☎ 3491-0111 [JR] Meguro Sta. [¥] BS10,197 BT16,695 [C] JCB, DN, VISA, MC, AMEX, others

GAJOEN KANKO HOTEL

SUIGETSU HOTEL/OHGAISO	31
水月ホテル/鷗外荘	B4

A combination hotel/inn set amid wonderful natural scenery. Ohgaiso, a business-type hotel, is named after the great novelist Ohgai Mori, with whom it is associated. The Suigetsu Hotel is a Japanese inn. The two form a single complex, which includes a natural hot spring bath.

3-3-21 Ikenohata, Taito-ku ☎ 3822-4611 [S] Nezu Sta. [¥] BS6,800 BT12,600 [C] JCB, DN, VISA, MC, AMEX

SAWANOYA RYOKAN	31
澤の屋旅館	A3

Located in the old *shitamachi* downtown area of Tokyo, this inn retains a full measure of traditional Japanese charm. There are also a variety of worthwhile sights in the neighborhood, including Ueno Park, the National Museum of Modern Art, and Ueno Zoo, Japan's first. Virtually all the guests are foreigners.

2-3-11 Yanaka, Taito-ku ☎ 3822-2251 [S] Nezu Sta. [¥] S4,000 T7,400 BT8,000 [C] AMEX

RYOKAN KATSUTARO	31
旅館勝太郎	B3

Highly recommended for an enjoyable stay in Tokyo's old downtown area. It's just a few minutes' walk to Ueno Zoo and Ueno Park, where you're likely to meet students from the Tokyo National University of Fine Arts and Music, which is also nearby. For runners, the neighborhood offers some outstanding jogging possibilities.

4-16-8 Ikenohata Taito-ku ☎ 3821-9808 [S] Nezu Sta. [¥] S3,900 BS4,400 T7,000 BT8,000 [C] VISA, MC, AMEX

RYOKAN MIKAWAYA BEKKAN	32
旅館三河屋別館	B3

A Japanese inn located near the famed Asakusa Kannon Temple in the heart of Asakusa, one of Japan's finest old downtown areas. An enjoyable part of your stay here will be slipping into the light, comfortable *kimono* provided to all guests. An excellent choice for anyone interested in the spirit of old Japan. Asakusa Kannon Temple, incidently, is a must-see for any visitor.

1-31-11 Asakusa, Taito-ku ☎ 3843-2345 [S] Asakusa Sta. [¥] S4,800 T9,200 [C] VISA, AMEX

SUKEROKU-NO-YADO SADACHIYO	32
助六の宿 貞千代	C3

For a complete, traditional Japanese experience, you could hardly do better than to stay here. Especially appealing is the bath, an authentic hot spring. Nothing is quite so relaxing at the end of a long day as a long hot soak in natural mineral water.

2-20-1 Asakusa, Taito-ku ☎ 3842-6431 [S] Asakusa Sta. [¥] 18,000 per person with meal

RYOKAN SANSUISO	−
旅館山水荘	−

Located near Gotanda Station, so extremely convenient for excursions to the Shibuya, Harajuku, and Aoyama areas. The neighborhood is relatively quiet, and the Meguro River is just outside your door. "Cleanliness creates its own atmosphere," says the friendly owner, and he clearly practices what he preaches.

2-9-5 Higashi-Gotanda, Shinagawa-ku ☎ 3441-7475 [JR] Gotanda Sta. [¥] S4,300 BS4,500 T8,000 BT8,400 [C] VISA, AMEX

KIKUYA RYOKAN	32
喜久屋旅館	B2

Ideally situated for viewing the old downtown area. The location, near Asakusa Kannon Temple, is convenient for getting around town. This gives you the choice of enjoying the traditional neighborhood around the inn, or hopping on the nearby train and going to the Ginza and Tokyo Station areas.

2-18-9 Nishi-Asakusa, Taito-ku ☎ 3841-6404 [S] Tawara-cho Sta. [¥] S4,000 BS4,600 T7,000 BT7,400-8,000 [C] VISA, MC, AMEX

SAKURA RYOKAN	31
桜旅館	D3

A new inn, opened only in 1989. Both Japanese-style and Western-style rooms are available, and all are impeccably clean. The location, near Asakusa Kannon Temple and Ueno Park, makes it a convenient base for outings. The neighborhood, quiet and still somewhat traditional, helps make for a relaxing stay.

2-6-2 Iriya, Taito-ku ☎ 3876-8118 [S] Iriya Sta. [¥] S4,500 BS5,500 T9,000 BT9,400 [C] AMEX

INABASO RYOKAN	27
稲葉荘旅館	H3

Situated at the very heart of Tokyo, this inn is a truly convenient base for shopping and sightseeing. The famed Hanazono Shrine is also nearby. Despite the neighborhood of large modern buildings, the inn itself maintains a relaxed — and relaxing — mood. When any of several annual local festivals are held, the street outside is lined with food and game stalls until well into the evening.

5-6-13 Shinjuku, Shinjuku-ku ☎ 3341-9581 [S] [JR] Shinjuku Sta. [¥] BS4,800 BT8,500 [C] VISA, AMEX

SOSHIGAYA HOT SPRING 21
そしがや温泉 21 Soshigaya onsen 21

The bath here is a natural hot spring, but open to the public for the same low rate as any ordinary public bathhouse. You have your choice of nine different types of baths. For an extra charge there is also a swimming pool. This "hot spring for the 21st Century," as it calls itself, attracts a good number of foreign visitors.

3-36-21 Soshigaya, Setagaya-ku ☎ 3483-2611 P Odakyu Line Soshigaya-Okura Sta. ⊙ 14:00-23:00 H None ¥ Adult 310 Child 150 C None

SOSHIGAYA HOT SPRING 21

RAKUTENCHI SAUNA | — |
楽天地サウナ | — |

You can't miss it: it's in the imposing building in front of Kinshi-cho Station on the Chuo train line. Tokyo's biggest bathhouse features a whole variety of baths, but the favorite is the sauna-with-a-view on the top floor. Come here in the evening to relax and rejuvenate while watching the lights of the city below.

4-27 Koto-bashi, Sumida-ku ☎ 3631-4126 JR Kinshi-cho Sta. ⊙ 10:00-23:30 (Sat. hol. -24:00) H None ¥ Men 2,400 Women 1,800 Child 1,050 C None

AZABU JUBAN HOT SPRING

AZABU JUBAN HOT SPRING | 21 |
麻布十番温泉 | Azabu Juban Onsen | G2 |

"Please be sure to bring a towel," says the owner of this well known hot spring, located in an upmarket Tokyo neighborhood. It's an ideal choice for anyone wanting to try a hot spring without venturing outside the city. The many embassies in the area help supply a steady foreign clientele, so even first-time bathers won't feel out of place. Well worth a visit.

1-5-22 Azabu-juban, Minato-ku ☎ 3404-2610 S Roppongi Sta. ⊙ 11:00-21:00 H Tue. ¥ Adult 1,200 Child 500 (18:00- Adult 800 Child 300) C None

RAKUTENCHI SAUNA

SAWANOYU | –
沢の湯 | –

Here you have a choice of four different baths: a sitting-style bath, a whirlpool type, an ultrasonic vibration bath, and a cool water bath. They also have a workout area for pre-bath exertions and a coffee shop, for after-bath refreshment.

2-26-18 Komamezawa, Itabashi-ku ☎ 3966-4497 Ⓢ Shimura-Sakaue Sta. 🕐 15:30-23:30 Ⓗ Mon. ¥ 310 Ⓒ None

NEW EBISU | –
ニュー恵美須 | –

Another bathhouse offering a good variety of different types of baths. Choices include long baths to stretch out in, ultrasonic, whirlpool, and low-frequency electric baths. But the piece de resistance is clearly the outdoor bath, complete with its own Japanese-style garden dotted with stone lanterns. A visit here will provide you with stories for years.

4-17-9 Higashi-Ogu, Arakawa-ku ☎ 3894-7602 Ⓙ Tabata Sta. 🕐 15:30-01:00 Ⓗ 1st & 3rd Mon. ¥ Adult 310 Child 150 Ⓒ None

YOSHIDA ACUPUNCTURE CLINIC | –
吉田温鍼院　Yoshida Onshin-in | –

This acupuncture clinic requires an appointment, so be sure to telephone before you visit. The treatment, which uses heated needles, is especially effective for sports-related injuries, earning the clinic a good reputation among student athletes. If you have tendon or other damage which hasn't responded to other treatments, this could well be the answer.

4-7-3 Todoroki, Setagaya-ku ☎ 3702-8989 Ⓟ Tokyu-Oimachi Line Todoroki Sta. 🕐 10:00-12:00, 14:00-18:00 Ⓗ Sun, & hol. ¥ First visit 6,000, From 2nd visit 4,000, Ⓒ None

HEIWAJIMA KURHAUS | 15
平和島クアハウス | F6

The attraction here is a choice of 13 different baths, each offering its own benefits. There is a natural hot spring bath, for example, as well as a round pool for water aerobics. Before your bath, work out in the training room, which is equipped with a number of machines and staffed by a trainer. After bathing, enjoy the lounge and video room. All this for ¥2,200 per adult. Recommended for our health-conscious readers.

1-1-1 Heiwajima, Ota-ku ☎ 3768-9121 Ⓟ Keihin-Kyuko Line Heiwajima Sta. Omori-kaigan Sta. 🕐 Weekdays 11:00-22:00, Weekends 10:00-22:00 Ⓗ None ¥ 2,200 Ⓒ None

HEIWAJIMA KURHAUS

CHOAN ACUPUNCTURE CLINIC | –
長安鍼灸院　Choan Shinkyu-in | –

Headed by a Chinese doctor with a background in orthopedic surgery, this clinic offers expert massage, acupuncture, moxibustion, and Chinese chiropractics. Patients come here from throughout Japan, as do a number of foreigners.

Ichinoe Bldg. 3F 4-2 Harue-cho, Edogawa-ku ☎ 3654-5592 Ⓢ Higashi-Ojima Sta. 🕐 09:00-13: 00, 15:00-19:00 Ⓗ Wed. ¥ First visit 4,000, From 2nd visit 3,500 Ⓒ None

YOYOGI PARK	22
代々木公園 Yoyogi Koen	D1

This spacious park, adjacent to Meiji Shrine, once served as training ground for the Imperial Army. Later it housed athletes for the 1964 Tokyo Olympics. Today it's popular — especially on weekends — for its grassy lawns, cherry trees, and paths for walking and cycling (rental bikes available). It's also a great place to jog. One newer attraction occurs each Sunday, when the road through the park is closed to traffic: a number of amateur rock bands set up and put on live performances. More than a few have gone on to professional careers after a start here.

JR Harajuku Sta. S Yoyogi-koen Sta.

YOYOGI PARK

YOYOGI NATIONAL STADIUM	22
代々木競技場 Kokuritsu Yoyogi Kyogijo	D1

Built for the 1964 Tokyo Olympics, this stadium features two 50-meter pools, with six and eight lanes respectively. The larger pool is open to the public from July 19 through August 24 only. The smaller pool is open year-round (but only on weekends during the above period.)

2-1-1 Jinnan, Shibuya-ku ☎ 3468-1171 JR Harajuku Sta. S Meiji-jingu-mae Sta. ⏰ Main Pool 10: 00-20:00 Sub Pool 12:00-17:00 (Sat.& hol. 10: 00-17:00) H 2nd & 4th Tue. ¥ Free Time:Adult 460 Child 360 C None

AROUND THE IMPERIAL PALACE	13
皇居周辺	E1

Some five kilometers long and traffic-free, the path surrounding the Imperial Palace is a mid-town Mecca for Tokyo joggers. You can start anywhere, but one recommendation is Sakuradamon (near S Sakuradamon Sta.), conveniently equipped with public toilets, water fountains, and a clock. On the first Sunday of each month the "Global Imperial Palace Marathon" is held here, with five different races ranging from five to 42 kilometers. Entry is ¥1,500 (¥2,000 for the 42 km. race). Call ☎ 3295-8460 for information.

S Sakuradamon Sta., Hanzomon Sta., Kudanshita Sta., Takebashi Sta., Nijubashi Sta.

AROUND THE IMPERIAL PALACE

NAKANO SUN PLAZA	—
中野サンプラザ	—

Attached to this concert hall is a sports complex including a seven-lane 25-meter heated pool. Note that the hours shown below vary according to the season, with longer hours during the summer months. Call to confirm times.

4-1-1 Nakano, Nakano-ku ☎ 3388-1151 S JR Nakano Sta. ⏰ Weekdays 17:00-21:40/ Sat. 10:00-21:40 Sun.12:00-19:40 H None ¥ 2 hrs: Adult 750 Child 500 C None

TOKYO SWIMMING CENTER　—

東京スイミングセンター　—

Offers twin 50m × 25m pools, one outside and one inside. The outdoor pool is open during the summer only, while the inside pool is heated for year-round use. Serious swimmers can purchase the "Summer Swim Card" (¥10,300), which allows unlimited admission during the month of July and August.

5-4-21 Komagome, Toshima-ku ☎ 3915-1012 ⒥⒭ Sugamo Sta. ◷ Tue. - Fri. 12:30-20:00/ Sun. & hol. 12:45-18:00 (times vary seasonally) Ⓗ Mon. ¥ Free Time:Adult 1,340 Child 720 Ⓒ None

SHOWA-NO-MORI TENNIS COURTS

SHOWA-NO-MORI TENNIS COURTS　15　F6

昭和の森テニスコート

A large tennis complex located in wooded surroundings on the outskirts of Tokyo. Use of the courts is by reservation only, so be sure to phone. Language should not be a problem: several of the staff speak English.

600 Tanaka-cho, Akishima-shi ☎ 0425-43-2103 ⒥⒭ Akishima Sta. ◷ 08:00-21:00 Ⓗ None ¥ Weekdays 2hrs.:1,250 Weekends 2hrs.:1,850 Ⓒ None

ARIAKE TENNIS FOREST PARK　15　H5

有明テニスの森公園Ariake Tenis-no-Mori Koen

A total of 48 clay and all-weather courts make this Tokyo's biggest tennis center. Fees are ¥1,300 per court per hour on weekdays, ¥1,500 on weekends and holidays. Reservations should be made by *ofuku hagaki* (postage-paid reply post cards, available at any post office) two to three months in advance.

2-5-1 Ariake, Koto-ku ☎ 3529-3301 Ⓢ Toyosu Sta. ◷ 09:00-21:00 (Nov. - Mar. -16:00) Ⓗ None Ⓒ None.

PUBLIC SPORTS FACILITIES

SIBUYA-KU SPORTS CENTER 渋谷区スポーツセンター	1-40-18 Nishihara, Shibuya-ku	☎3468-9051	Swimming,Ping-pong, Tennis, Jymnasium, Basketball, Volleyball, Jogging, baseball　**22・B6**
MINATO-KU SPORTS CENTER 港区スポーツセンター	3-1-19 Shibaura, Minato-ku	☎3452-4151	Swimming, Ping-pong, Jymnasium, Basketball, Volleyball, Jogging　**15・F2**
CHIYODA JYMNASIUM 千代田体育館	2-1-8 Uchi-Kanda, Chiyoda-ku	☎3256-8444	Swimming, Ping-pong, Jymnasium, Basketball, Volleyball　**12・H2**
SHINJUKU SPORTS CENTER 新宿スポーツセンター	3-5-1 Okubo, Shinjuku-ku	☎3232-7701	Swimming, Ping-pong, Jymnasium, Basketball, Volleyball　**27・H1**

ACCOMMODATION & HEALTH

Home Visit System

For anyone truly wanting a better understanding of Japan and things Japanese, perhaps the single most valuable experience is a visit to a typical home. This is the idea behind the Home Visit System, a program that provides a chance to spend a few hours with an ordinary Japanese family in their own home. Many foreign guests have praised the program, saying that it has left pleasant and indelible memories of Japan. A total of 1,190 families nationwide have volunteered to host these visits, of which 65 are in Tokyo. Most speak English, and some can converse in French and German as well.

● Advice for Home Visits

It is important that guests arrive at the home of their host family at the day and time scheduled. A small gift or souvenir of your own country makes a thoughtful way to express your appreciation. Most visits are scheduled for the evening hours, after dinner, so you are likely to be served tea and perhaps sweets, but no meal. Enjoy your visit, and don't feel you have to ask any overly formal or academic questions about Japanese culture or customs.

● Requesting a Visit

The Home Visit System operates in 17 cities around Japan, including Tokyo, Osaka, and Kyoto. Requests for visits in Tokyo can be made by telephone or mail, as shown below (note that the telephone service does not operate on Sundays or holidays). For the convenience of the host family, please make your request at least one day before your desired date of visit, and preferably as early as possible. Any special language needs or other requirements should be made clear when you make your request.

USEFUL
INFORMATION

Telephone Service

● Public Telephones

Public telephones can be found along the streets throughout Tokyo. Most are green, though you will occasionally also see red or yellow ones. The green color signifies the latest models, most of which accept both coins and telephone cards (though some take cards only). Telephone cards —— prepaid magnetic-backed cards —— are available in ¥500, ¥1,000, ¥3,000, and ¥5,000 denominations, and can be bought at train station kiosks and many other places. Red public telephones accept ¥10 coins only; yellow phones, both ¥10 and ¥100 coins. Neither take telephone cards.

Whatever the color, public telephones in Japan are operated the same way as in most other countries. First pick up the receiver, insert either one or more coins or a telephone card, then dial the number you want to call (usually by push-button, though a few rotary-type dials remain). When calling another Tokyo number from within the city, there is no need to dial the 03 prefix. Calls to areas outside of Tokyo require you to first dial an area code. Should your coins or card run out during the call, you'll hear a beeping signal, giving you a few seconds to insert more coins or a new card.

● International Calls

Three companies now provide overseas telephone services from Japan: KDD, IDC, and ITJ. Each is accessed by a different prefix, and each has a different system of rates. Below is an example of direct dialing to New York using KDD.

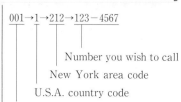

001→1→212→123－4567

Number you wish to call
New York area code
U.S.A. country code
KDD international direct dialing service access number
(0061 for IDC, 0041 for ITJ)

Country Codes

U S A, Canada	1	Philippines	63
France	33	Rep. of Korea	82
United Kingdom	44	China	86
Germany	49	Hong Kong	852
Australia	61	Taiwan	886

Station-to-station, person-to-person, collect, and credit card calls are available. Reach the operator by dialing 0051 for KDD. Operator-Assisted Calls is used only KDD.

Postal Service

Stamped postcards and letters can be posted at any red mailbox. Packages should be taken to a post office for mailing. Postal services are also available at the front desks of most hotels. Rates within Japan are ¥62 for letters up to 25 grams in weight, ¥72 for up to 50 grams (letter sizes from 9 × 14 cm to 12 × 23.5 cm). Domestic postcards are ¥41. Air Mail Rates

	Asia	North & Central Americas, Oceania, Near & Middle East	Europe, Africa, South America
Postcards	¥70	¥70	¥70
Aerograms	¥80	¥80	¥80
Letters(Up to 10g)	¥80	¥100	¥120
(Up to 20g)	¥140	¥170	¥220

Business Hours

● Banks
Bank tellers and ATMs (automated teller machines) operate different hours in Japan, as shown below.

	Tellers	ATMs
Weekdays	9am.-3pm.	9am.-7pm.
Saturdays	Closed	9am.-5pm.
Sundays	Closed	Closed

● Post Offices
Weekdays: 9 am. - 5 pm. (Some post offices close at 7 pm.) Saturdays: 9 am. - 3 pm. (Some post offices until 5 pm.) Sundays: Closed

● Government Offices and Companies
Government offices are generally open from 9 am. to 5 pm., Monday through Friday only. Most companies are open from about 9 am. to 5 or 6 pm. on weekdays, and until noon on Saturdays. Almost all firms are closed on Sundays and national holidays.

● Shops
Most department stores open at 10 am. and close at 7 pm. Each store customarily takes one day off per week, most often Wednesday or Thursday (except at year-end and other busy seasons, when they are open every day). Other types of stores vary in their business hours, but generally open about 10 am. and close around 8 pm. Shops in Japan do not close for a noontime break.

Tourist Information Center	12
	D2

(Japan National Tourist Organization) The Tourist Information Center provides a wide range of free services to travellers visiting Japan. These include distribution of free pamphlets and other sightseeing information, recommendations regarding travel in Japan, and assistance with any problems or difficulties encountered by tourists. Please feel free to make use of these services.

Tokyo Office: Kotani Bldg., 1-6-6 Yurakucho, Chiyoda-ku
☎ 3502-1461(for callers within Tokyo)
☎ 0120-222-800 (toll-free number for callers from outside Tokyo)
Telephone service: 9:00-17:00(year-round)
Information counter: 9:00- 17:00 (Mon.- Fri.),
9:00 - 12:00 (Sat.)
Closed Sun., Hol.
JNTO Tourist Information Center Tokyo Office: Kotani Bldg., 1-6-6 Yurakucho, Chiyoda-ku ☎ 3502-1461

Air lines

Japan Air Lines　for domestic ·······································5489-2111
　　　　　　　　　for International ·······························5489-1111
All Nippon Airways　for domestic ·······························5489-8800
　　　　　　　　　　for International ····························3272-1212
Japan Air System for domestic　······························3432-6111
　　　　　　　　　for International ·······························3438-1155
Air France　···3475-1511
Air New Zealand ··3287-1641
American Airlines ··3214-2111
British Airways···3593-8811
Canadian Airlines International·······································3281-7426
Cathay Pacific Airlines ··3504-1531
Continental Airlines ···3592-1631
Delta Airlines ···5275-7000
Korean Air Lines ··3211-3311
Lufthansa German Airlines　··3580-2111
Northwest Orient Airlines···3432-6000
Qantas Airways　··3593-7000
Singapore Airlines···3213-3431
United Airlines···3817-4411
Virgin Atlantic Airways··3435-8330

Lost and Found
JR
Tokyo Station Lost-and-Found Office ·································3231-1880
Ueno Station Lost-and-Found Office　······························3841-8069
Subway
Eidan Subway Lost-and-Found Office ·································3834-5577
Toei Subway Lost-and-Found Office　·······························3818-5760
Taxi
Tokyo Taxi Kindaika Center ··3648-0300

Railways

JR Information Center	3212-4441
Keio Teito Electric Railway	3356-3111
Keisei Electric Raiway	3831-0131
Odakyu Electric Railway	3349-2000
Seibu Railway	0429-26-2221
Tobu Railway	3621-5206
Tokyu Corporation	3477-6111
Teito Rapid Transit Authority (Eidan)	3837-7111
The Metropolitan Subway (Toei)	5600-2020

Emergency

Police	110
Fire/Ambulance	119

Hospitals

National Medical Center Hospital	3202-7181
2nd Tokyo National Hospital	3411-0111
Japan Red Cross Medical Center	3400-1311
St. Luke's International Hospital	3541-5151
Toranomon Hospital	3588-1111
University of Tokyo Hospital	3815-5411
Keio University Hospital	3353-1211

Credit Cards

JCB Co.,Ltd.	3294-8111
Diners Club of Japan	3499-1311
Visa Int.	3503-6951
Master Card Japan	5256-6951
American Express Int. Inc.	3220-6200

Others

Telephone Information	104
Telephone Repair	113
Teletourist Service (English)	3503-2911
Teletourist Service (French)	3503-2926

USEFULINFORMATION

INDEX

S

T

For Your Travelife **JTB**

TRAVEL GUIDE TOKYO TODAY

〈英文東京おもしろガイド〉

初版印刷　1991年1月1日
初版発行　1991年1月15日
　　　　　(Jan.15, 1991 1st edition)
編 集 人　中嶋隆一
発 行 人　内藤錦樹
発 行 所　JTB日本交通公社出版事業局
　　　　　〒101　東京都千代田区神田鍛冶町3-3　大木ビル8階
印 刷 所　交通印刷株式会社

編　　集　JTB海外ガイドブック編集部 (Tel.03-3257-8391)
制作協力　株式会社アーバン・トランスレーション
地図協力　山口清知
イラスト　角 新作
写真協力　株式会社リーワード
翻　　訳　Julia Nolet, Martha Chaiklin
　　　　　,Urban Connections Inc.

JTB発行図書のご注文は
JTB出版販売センター
〒101 東京都千代田区神田須田町1-28タイムビル3階 (Tel.03-3257-8337)

903820 711050

ISBN4-533-01648-0

Meet Japan Through

SUNRISE TOURS *JTB*

The Japan Travel Bureau operates its famed Sunrise Tours to a wide variety of destinations, including Tokyo, Nikko, Hakone, Mt. Fuji, Kyoto, the Inland Sea, Kyushu, etc. Let JTB host you to the best of Japan. Pick-up services are available from major hotels.

Sights in Tokyo	
● Tokyo Morning	¥3,910
● Tokyo Afternoon	¥4,450
● Dynamic Tokyo Full Day	¥9,980

Special interest tours	
Adventures into Japanese arts and crafts, industrial technology, and rural life.	¥10,300

Night tours	
● Tokyo Kabuki Night	¥12,970
● Tokyo Fascinating Night	¥11,050
● Tokyo Bright Night	¥8,970

Short excursions from Tokyo	
● Nikko	¥18,500
● Kamakura·Hakone	¥15,000 & ¥18,500
● Mt.Fuji·Hakone	¥15,000 & ¥18,500
● Kyoto trips	¥46,500 and up

The above are only part of JTB's huge assortment of Sunrise Tours.

Fares are effective as of January 1, 1991.

For information and reservations,
Call any day Tokyo 3276-7777 (9:00 a.m.—8:30 p.m.)

JAPAN TRAVEL BUREAU, Inc.
LICENSED TRAVEL AGENT No.64
International Travel Div., 1-13-1 Nihombashi, Tokyo 103, Japan